The Super Easy Keto Diet Cookbook

1500 Days of Carb-Conscious Cuisine Using the Metric Measurements / Full Colour Edition

Matilda Nicholson

Copyright© 2024 By Matilda Nicholson Rights Reserved

This book is copyright protected. It is only for personal use. You cannot amend, distribute, sell, use, quote or paraphrase any part of the content within this book, without the consent of the author or publisher.

Under no circumstances will any blame or legal responsibility be held against the publisher, or author, for any damages, reparation, or monetary loss due to the information contained within this book, either directly or indirectly.

Disclaimer Notice:

Please note the information contained within this document is for educational and entertainment purposes only. All effort has been executed to present accurate, up to date, reliable, complete information. No warranties of any kind are declared or implied. Readers acknowledge that the author is not engaged in the rendering of legal, financial, medical or professional advice. The content within this book has been derived from various sources. Please consult a licensed professional before attempting any techniques outlined in this book.

By reading this document, the reader agrees that under no circumstances is the author responsible for any losses, direct or indirect, that are incurred as a result of the use of the information contained within this document, including, but not limited to, errors, omissions, or inaccuracies.

Editor: AALIYAH LYONS

Interior Design: BROOKE WHITE

Cover Art: DANIELLE REES

Food stylist: SIENNA ADAMS

Table Of Contents

Introduction	1
Chapter 1	
The Keto Lifestyle Unveiled	**2**
Discovering the Essence of Keto Diet	3
Essential Staples for a British Keto Pantry	3
Eat & Avoid Guide	5
Chapter 2	
4-Week Meal Plan	**9**
Week 1	10
Week 2	10
Week 3	11
Week 4	11

Chapter 3	
Breakfast	**13**
Ham, Cheese and Egg Cups	14
Breakfast Egg Muffins	14
Cheesy Brussels Sprouts	15
Double-Pork Frittata	15
Indian Masala Frittata	16
Bacon Deviled Eggs	16
Bacon-Wrapped Avocado Fries	17
Paprika Egg Salad	17
Tart with Broccoli and Greek Yogurt	18
Mini Frittatas with Sausage and Goat Cheese	18

Chapter 4
Snacks and Appetizers — 19
Provolone Cheese Chips with Herbs — 20
Cheesy Chicken and Ham Bites — 20
Greek-Style Ricotta Dip with Olives — 21
Favorite Onions Rings — 21
Italian Cheese Crisps — 22
Double Cheese Bites — 22
Mouth-Watering Stuffed Mushrooms — 23
Fudge Bars with Almonds — 23
Mediterranean-Style Keto Sticks — 24
Rum Chocolate Chip Cookies — 24
Easy Classic Cheesecake — 25
Vanilla Custard Pudding — 25
Mom's Coffee Fudge — 26

Chapter 5
Poultry — 27
Old-Fashioned Chicken Soup — 28
Lemon Garlic Grilled Chicken Wings — 28
Italian-Seasoned Turkey Breasts — 29
Pan-Fried Meatballs — 29
Buttery Garlic Chicken — 30
Roast Chicken with Olives — 30
Parmesan Baked Chicken — 31
Cheesy Jalapeño Chicken — 31
Green Chicken Curry — 32
Coconut Chicken Tenders — 32

Chapter 6
Beef, Lamb and Pork — 33
Sunday Pot Roast with Vegetable Mash — 34
Cheesy and Buttery Pork Chops — 34
Paprika Crusted Pork Cutlets — 35
Christmas Chuck Eye Roast — 35
Bacon, Pork and Cabbage Skillet — 36
Easy Jerk Ribs — 36
Restaurant-Style Burger Patties — 37
Classic Oven Pot Roast — 37
Sweet Beef Curry — 38
Pork Fillets with Mustard Sauce — 38
BBQ Beef & Slaw — 39

Chapter 7
Fish and Seafood — 40
Baked Lemon-Butter Fish — 41
Creamy Dill Salmon — 41
Sautéed Pesto Mahi Mahi — 42
Grilled Garlic-Lemon Prawns — 42
Grilled Salmon with Dijon Glaze — 43
Shrimp Scampi with Courgette Noodles — 43
Garlic Butter Prawns — 44
Baked Cod with Herbed Butter — 44
Grilled Salmon with Dijon-Honey Glaze — 45
Lemon Herb Butter Shrimp — 45

Chapter 8
Vegan and Vegetarian — 46
Radical Radish Chips — 47
Cauliflower and Broccoli Bake — 47
Mixed-Vegetable Lasagna — 48
Vegan Avocado and Courgette Noodles — 48
Baked Courgette Fries — 49
Carrot-Pumpkin Pudding — 49
Cheesy Broccoli — 50
Vegan Coconut Curry with Tofu — 50
Roasted Radishes — 51
Keto Aubergine Parmesan — 51

Chapter 9
Soups, Stew and Salads — 52
Pan-Fried Egg Salad — 53
Creamy Cucumber Avocado Soup — 53
Shrimp Caprese Salad — 54
Shrimp and Avocado Salad — 54
Creamy Tomato-Basil Soup — 55
Cabbage Detox Soup — 55
Cajun Shrimp Salad — 56
Blue Cheese and Bacon Kale Salad — 56
Cheeseburger Salad — 57
Taco Soup — 57

Appendix 1 Measurement Conversion Chart — 58
Appendix 2 The Dirty Dozen and Clean Fifteen — 60
Appendix 3 Index — 62

Introduction

In the realm of culinary delight and mindful nourishment, the Super British Keto Diet Cookbook awaits you—an exquisite journey into the fusion of traditional British flavors and the innovative spirit of the ketogenic lifestyle. As you embark on this gastronomic adventure, allow me to extend an invitation into a world where health-conscious choices intertwine seamlessly with the vibrant tapestry of British culinary heritage.

Amid the hustle and bustle of our daily lives, finding a balance between flavor and nutrition can be a challenge. The British Keto Diet not only rises to meet this challenge but does so with an elegant dance of taste and well-being. Within the pages of this cookbook, a symphony of carefully crafted recipes awaits, offering a harmonious blend of traditional British favorites and the healthful principles of Keto living.

This collection is more than a mere assortment of recipes; it's a holistic guide to embracing a lifestyle that nurtures your body and soul. Each dish is an exploration of local, seasonal ingredients, a celebration of the simplicity and richness that British cuisine has to offer, reinvented through the lens of Keto wisdom.

What sets the Super British Keto Diet Cookbook apart is its commitment to accessibility. No exotic or hard-to-find ingredients; just a celebration of the flavors that the British countryside has to offer. With a touch of creativity, you'll discover that Keto living is not only attainable but a delicious journey through familiar tastes.

The recipes featured here are more than a culinary guide; they're an invitation to explore the diverse palette of British flavors, expertly reimagined for the Keto lifestyle. Whether you're a seasoned Keto enthusiast or a newcomer to the practice, each dish is designed to be a source of inspiration—a canvas for your culinary creativity.

So, whether you're savoring the delicate aroma of a Keto-friendly shepherd's pie or indulging in the richness of a low-carb sticky toffee pudding, let each bite be a reminder that you're not just nourishing your body; you're engaging in the joy of mindful eating. The Super British Keto Diet Cookbook is your compass on this journey, guiding you toward a healthier, more flavorful way of living—one delicious meal at a time.

May your culinary exploration be filled with joy, discovery, and the satisfaction of nourishing yourself in the most delightful way. Cheers to your health, happiness, and the exciting adventure that awaits within these pages!

Chapter 1

The Keto Lifestyle Unveiled

Discovering the Essence of Keto Diet

Embarking on the journey of discovering the essence of the Keto diet is not merely a quest for weight loss; it's a transformative exploration of a lifestyle that champions health, satiety, and sustainable well-being. At its core, the Keto diet is a low-carbohydrate, high-fat dietary approach designed to shift the body's primary energy source from carbohydrates to fats. Let's delve into the practical aspects that make the Keto diet not just a trend but a profound and effective way of nourishing the body.

UNDERSTANDING THE FUNDAMENTALS:
The Keto diet revolves around a fundamental principle—reducing carbohydrate intake and increasing fat consumption. This triggers a metabolic state known as ketosis, where the body efficiently burns stored fats for energy. Carbohydrates, the body's primary fuel source, are limited, leading to a significant reduction in blood sugar levels and insulin production.

PRACTICAL BENEFITS:
- Weight Management: One of the most tangible and sought-after outcomes of the Keto diet is weight management. By shifting the body's energy source to fats, it becomes highly efficient at burning stored fat, leading to weight loss. However, the practicality lies in its sustainability. Unlike restrictive diets that often lead to rebound weight gain, the Keto lifestyle can be maintained over the long term.
- Enhanced Satiety: Unlike some traditional low-fat diets, the Keto diet emphasizes satisfying, nutrient-dense fats that contribute to a prolonged feeling of fullness. Practicality here is evident in the reduced likelihood of succumbing to between-meal cravings, making it easier to adhere to a controlled eating schedule.
- Stabilized Energy Levels: By eliminating the rollercoaster of blood sugar spikes and crashes associated with high-carb diets, the Keto diet provides a more stable and sustained energy supply. This practical benefit is particularly advantageous for those seeking improved focus, increased productivity, and enhanced physical performance throughout the day.
- Mental Clarity and Cognitive Function: The brain thrives on a steady supply of ketones, a byproduct of fat metabolism during ketosis. Many individuals on the Keto diet report improved mental clarity, heightened focus, and enhanced cognitive function. This practical advantage is invaluable in a world where mental acuity is often paramount.

Essential Staples for a British Keto Pantry

Building a British Keto pantry is the cornerstone of successfully navigating the culinary landscape of this unique dietary approach. As you embark on your Keto journey infused with the essence of British flavors, stocking your pantry with essential staples becomes an artful and practical undertaking. Let's explore the practicality behind choosing and maintaining these ingredients to create flavorful and satisfying Keto meals.

FOUNDATIONS OF A BRITISH KETO PANTRY:
- Quality Fats: At the heart of the Keto diet lies a focus on healthy fats. Avocado oil, olive oil, and coconut oil are versatile options for cooking and dressing. These not only serve as a rich source of healthy fats but also impart a delightful depth of flavor to your dishes.

- Lean Proteins: Sourcing lean proteins is crucial for a well-rounded Keto diet. Include staples like grass-fed beef, free-range chicken, and wild-caught fish in your pantry. These proteins not only provide essential nutrients but also align with the commitment to quality and sustainability.
- Low-Carb Flour Alternatives: For those moments when the baking bug bites, having almond flour and coconut flour on hand is a practical choice. These low-carb alternatives open up a world of possibilities for creating Keto-friendly baked goods, from bread to desserts, without compromising on taste or texture.
- Nuts and Seeds: Almonds, walnuts, chia seeds, and flaxseeds are excellent additions to a British Keto pantry. These provide a crunchy texture to meals, serve as snack options, and contribute healthy fats, fiber, and essential nutrients to your diet.

PRACTICAL CONSIDERATIONS FOR PANTRY MAINTENANCE:

- Storage Solutions: To ensure the longevity of your pantry staples, invest in airtight containers. This not only keeps ingredients fresh but also helps you stay organized, making meal preparation a more efficient and enjoyable process.
- Regular Inventory Checks: Practicality lies in maintaining a well-organized pantry. Regularly check expiration dates and replenish items as needed. This not only prevents food waste but also ensures that you have the necessary ingredients at your fingertips when inspiration strikes.
- Seasonal Varieties: Embrace the practicality of seasonal eating by incorporating fresh produce into your Keto pantry. While certain items may be stored for the long term, integrating seasonal vegetables and herbs adds vibrancy and nutritional diversity to your meals.
- Readily Available Condiments: Stocking up on Keto-friendly condiments is a practical way to add flavor without compromising your dietary goals. Mustard, sugar-free ketchup, and various herbs and spices can transform a simple dish into a culinary masterpiece.

Eat & Avoid Guide

KETO FOODS TO ENJOY

HIGH FAT / LOW CARB (BASED ON NET CARBS)

MEATS & SEAFOOD
- Beef (ground beef, steak, etc.)
- Chicken
- Crab
- Crawfish
- Duck
- Fish
- Goose
- Lamb
- Lobster
- Mussels
- Octopus
- Pork (pork chops, bacon, etc.)
- Quail
- Sausage (without fillers)
- Scallops
- Shrimp
- Veal
- Venison

DAIRY
- Blue cheese dressing
- Burrata cheese
- Cottage cheese
- Cream cheese
- Eggs
- Greek yogurt (full-fat)
- Grilling cheese
- Halloumi cheese
- Heavy (whipping) cream
- Kefalotyri cheese
- Mozzarella cheese
- Provolone cheese
- Queso blanco
- Ranch dressing
- Ricotta cheese
- Unsweetened almond milk
- Unsweetened coconut milk

VEGETABLES
- Alfalfa sprouts
- Asparagus
- Avocados
- Bell peppers
- Broccoli
- Cabbage
- Carrots (in moderation)
- Cauliflower
- Celery
- Chicory
- Coconut
- Cucumbers
- Garlic (in moderation)
- Green beans
- Herbs
- Jicama
- Lemons
- Limes
- Mushrooms
- Okra
- Olives
- Onions (in moderation)
- Pickles
- Pumpkin
- Radishes
- Salad greens
- Scallions
- Spaghetti squash (in moderation)
- Tomatoes (in moderation)
- Zucchini

NUTS & SEEDS
- Almonds
- Brazil nuts
- Chia seeds
- Flaxseeds
- Hazelnuts
- Macadamia nuts
- Peanuts (in moderation)
- Pecans
- Pine nuts
- Pumpkin seeds
- Sacha inchi seeds
- Sesame seeds
- Walnuts

FRUITS
- Blackberries
- Blueberries
- Cranberries
- Raspberries
- Strawberries

KETO FOODS TO AVOID

LOW FAT / HIGH CARB (BASED ON NET CARBS)

MEATS & MEAT ALTERNATIVES
- Deli meat (some, not all)
- Hot dogs (with fillers)
- Sausage (with fillers)
- Seitan
- Tofu

DAIRY
- Almond milk (sweetened)
- Coconut milk (sweetened)
- Milk
- Soy milk (regular)
- Yogurt (regular)

NUTS & SEEDS
- Cashews
- Chestnuts
- Pistachios

VEGETABLES
- Artichokes
- Beans (all varieties)
- Burdock root
- Butternut squash
- Chickpeas
- Corn
- Edamame
- Eggplant
- Leeks
- Parsnips
- Plantains
- Potatoes
- Sweet potatoes
- Winter squash
- Oranges
- Yams

FRUITS &
- Apples
- Apricots
- Bananas
- Boysenberries
- Cantaloupe
- Cherries
- Currants
- Dates
- Elderberries
- Gooseberries
- Grapes
- Honeydew melon
- Huckleberries
- Kiwifruits
- Taro root
- Turnips
- Mangos
- Peaches
- Peas
- Pineapples
- Plums
- Prunes
- Raisins
- Water chestnuts

KETO COOKING STAPLES
1. Pink Himalayan salt
2. Freshly ground black pepper
3. 3 Ghee (clarified butter, without dairy; buy
4. grass-fed if you can)
5. 4 Olive oil
6. Grass-fed butter

KETO PERISHABLES
Eggs (pasture-raised, if you can)
2 Avocados
3 Bacon (uncured)
Cream cheese (full-fat; or use a dairy-free alterna- tive)
Sour cream (full-fat; or use a dairy-free alternative)
Heavy whipping cream or coconut milk (full-fat; I buy the coconut milk in a can)
Garlic (fresh or pre-minced in a jar)
Meat (grass-fed, if you can)
10 Greens (spinach, kale, or arugula)

Chapter 2

4-Week Meal Plan

Week 1

DAY 1:
- Breakfast: Breakfast Egg Muffins
- Lunch: Easy Jerk Ribs
- Snack: Rum Chocolate Chip Cookies
- Dinner: Mixed-Vegetable Lasagna

Total for the day:
Calories: 4482;Fat: 298.5g;Carbs: 70.8g;Protein: 366.6g;Fiber: 21.3g

DAY 2:
- Breakfast: Breakfast Egg Muffins
- Lunch: Easy Jerk Ribs
- Snack: Rum Chocolate Chip Cookies
- Dinner: Mixed-Vegetable Lasagna

Total for the day:
Calories: 4482;Fat: 298.5g;Carbs: 70.8g;Protein: 366.6g;Fiber: 21.3g

DAY 3:
- Breakfast: Breakfast Egg Muffins
- Lunch: Easy Jerk Ribs
- Snack: Rum Chocolate Chip Cookies
- Dinner: Mixed-Vegetable Lasagna

Total for the day:
Calories: 4482;Fat: 298.5g;Carbs: 70.8g;Protein: 366.6g;Fiber: 21.3g

DAY 4:
- Breakfast: Double-Pork Frittata
- Lunch: Easy Jerk Ribs
- Snack: Rum Chocolate Chip Cookies
- Dinner: Mixed-Vegetable Lasagna

Total for the day:
Calories: 5054;Fat: 429.5g;Carbs: 94.7g;Protein: 440g;Fiber: 29.2g

DAY 5:
- Breakfast: Double-Pork Frittata
- Lunch: Mixed-Vegetable Lasagna
- Snack: Rum Chocolate Chip Cookies
- Dinner: Mixed-Vegetable Lasagna

Total for the day:
Calories: 8779;Fat: 791.5g;Carbs: 168.4g;Protein: 624.2g;Fiber: 51.9g

Week 2

DAY 1:
- Breakfast: Paprika Egg Salad
- Lunch: Roast Chicken with Olives
- Snack: Greek-Style Ricotta Dip with Olives
- Dinner: Restaurant-Style Burger Patties

Total for the day:
Calories: 2147;Fat: 118.4g;Carbs: 26.2g;Protein: 234.7g;Fiber: 5.3g

DAY 2:
- Breakfast: Paprika Egg Salad
- Lunch: Roast Chicken with Olives
- Snack: Greek-Style Ricotta Dip with Olives
- Dinner: Restaurant-Style Burger Patties

Total for the day:
Calories: 2147;Fat: 118.4g;Carbs: 26.2g;Protein: 234.7g;Fiber: 5.3g

DAY 3:
- Breakfast: Paprika Egg Salad
- Lunch: Roast Chicken with Olives
- Snack: Greek-Style Ricotta Dip with Olives
- Dinner: Restaurant-Style Burger Patties

Total for the day:
Calories: 2147;Fat: 118.4g;Carbs: 26.2g;Protein: 234.7g;Fiber: 5.3g

DAY 4:
- Breakfast: Paprika Egg Salad
- Lunch: Restaurant-Style Burger Patties
- Snack: Greek-Style Ricotta Dip with Olives

- Dinner: Roast Chicken with Olives

Total for the day:

Calories: 2147;Fat: 118.4g;Carbs: 26.2g;Protein: 234.7g;Fiber: 5.3g

DAY 5:

- Breakfast: Paprika Egg Salad
- Lunch: Restaurant-Style Burger Patties
- Snack: Greek-Style Ricotta Dip with Olives
- Dinner: Roast Chicken with Olives

Total for the day:

Calories: 2147;Fat: 118.4g;Carbs: 26.2g;Protein: 234.7g;Fiber: 5.3g

Week 3

DAY 1:

- Breakfast: Ham, Cheese and Egg Cups
- Lunch: Christmas Chuck Eye Roast
- Snack: Mom's Coffee Fudge
- Dinner: Carrot-Pumpkin Pudding

Total for the day:

Calories: 3055;Fat: 183.4g;Carbs: 44.5g;Protein: 297.8g;Fiber: 10.1g

DAY 2:

- Breakfast: Ham, Cheese and Egg Cups
- Lunch: Christmas Chuck Eye Roast
- Snack: Mom's Coffee Fudge
- Dinner: Carrot-Pumpkin Pudding

Total for the day:

Calories: 3055;Fat: 183.4g;Carbs: 44.5g;Protein: 297.8g;Fiber: 10.1g

DAY 3:

- Breakfast: Ham, Cheese and Egg Cups
- Lunch: Christmas Chuck Eye Roast
- Snack: Mom's Coffee Fudge
- Dinner: Carrot-Pumpkin Pudding

Total for the day:

Calories: 3055;Fat: 183.4g;Carbs: 44.5g;Protein: 297.8g;Fiber: 10.1g

DAY 4:

- Breakfast: Ham, Cheese and Egg Cups
- Lunch: Carrot-Pumpkin Pudding
- Snack: Mom's Coffee Fudge
- Dinner: Christmas Chuck Eye Roast

Total for the day:

Calories: 3055;Fat: 183.4g;Carbs: 44.5g;Protein: 297.8g;Fiber: 10.1g

DAY 5:

- Breakfast: Ham, Cheese and Egg Cups
- Lunch: Carrot-Pumpkin Pudding
- Snack: Mom's Coffee Fudge
- Dinner: Christmas Chuck Eye Roast

Total for the day:

Calories: 3055;Fat: 183.4g;Carbs: 44.5g;Protein: 297.8g;Fiber: 10.1g

Week 4

DAY 1:

- Breakfast: Bacon Deviled Eggs
- Lunch: Italian-Seasoned Turkey Breasts
- Snack: Cheesy Chicken and Ham Bites
- Dinner: Paprika Crusted Pork Cutlets

Total for the day:

Calories: 1371;Fat: 67.7g;Carbs: 18.4g;Protein: 164.8g;Fiber: 3.3g

DAY 2:

- Breakfast: Bacon Deviled Eggs
- Lunch: Italian-Seasoned Turkey Breasts
- Snack: Cheesy Chicken and Ham Bites
- Dinner: Paprika Crusted Pork Cutlets

Total for the day:

Calories: 1371;Fat: 67.7g;Carbs: 18.4g;Protein: 164.8g;Fiber: 3.3g

DAY 3:
- Breakfast: Bacon Deviled Eggs
- Lunch: Italian-Seasoned Turkey Breasts
- Snack: Cheesy Chicken and Ham Bites
- Dinner: Paprika Crusted Pork Cutlets

Total for the day:
Calories: 1371;Fat: 67.7g;Carbs: 18.4g;Protein: 164.8g;Fiber: 3.3g

DAY 4:
- Breakfast: Bacon Deviled Eggs
- Lunch: Paprika Crusted Pork Cutlets
- Snack: Cheesy Chicken and Ham Bites
- Dinner: Italian-Seasoned Turkey Breasts

Total for the day:
Calories: 1371;Fat: 67.7g;Carbs: 18.4g;Protein: 164.8g;Fiber: 3.3g

DAY 5:
- Breakfast: Bacon Deviled Eggs
- Lunch: Paprika Crusted Pork Cutlets
- Snack: Cheesy Chicken and Ham Bites
- Dinner: Italian-Seasoned Turkey Breasts

Total for the day:
Calories: 1371;Fat: 67.7g;Carbs: 18.4g;Protein: 164.8g;Fiber: 3.3g

Chapter 3

Breakfast

Ham, Cheese and Egg Cups

Prep time: 5 minutes | Cook time: 30 minutes |Serves 6

- 6 thin slices ham
- 1 teaspoon mustard
- 6 eggs
- 113 grams cream cheese
- 1/2 teaspoon red pepper flakes, crushed
- 170 grams Colby cheese, shredded

1. Spritz a muffin tin with nonstick cooking spray. Place the ham slices over each muffin cup and gently press down until a cup shape forms.
2. In a mixing dish, whisk the mustard, eggs, cream cheese, red pepper, garlic salt, and black pepper.
3. Transfer the muffin tin to a wire rack before serving. Garnish with spring onions and serve. Enjoy!

PER SERVING

Calories: 258 | Fat: 19.1g | Carbs: 2.8g | Protein: 17.5g | Fiber: 0.2g

Breakfast Egg Muffins

Prep time: 5 minutes | Cook time:20 minutes |Serves 4

- 6 tablespoons almond flour
- 2 tablespoons flaxseed meal
- 1/4 teaspoon baking soda
- 4 eggs
- 113 grams cheddar cheese, shredded

1. In a mixing bowl, thoroughly combine all of the above ingredients until well incorporated.
2. Line a muffin tin with non-stick baking cups. Scrape the batter into the prepared baking cups.
3. Bake in the preheated oven at 180 degrees Celsius (about 350 degrees Fahrenheit) for 15 to 17 minutes.
4. Transfer to a wire rack to cool slightly before unmolding and serving. Enjoy!

PER SERVING

Calories: 292 | Fat: 23.1g | Carbs: 5.4g | Protein: 16.4g | Fiber: 3.3g

Cheesy Brussels Sprouts

Prep time: 5 minutes | Cook time: 25 minutes | Serves 4

- 340 grams Brussels sprouts, cleaned and halved
- 2 tablespoons sesame oil
- 1 teaspoon dried parsley flakes
- 1 sprig dried thyme
- Sea salt and ground black pepper, to taste
- 170 grams Cheddar cheese, shredded

1. Start by preheating your oven to 200 degrees Celsius (about 392 degrees Fahrenheit).
2. Lightly grease a baking pan with non-stick cooking spray. Arrange the Brussels sprouts on the baking pan. Drizzle them with sesame oil.
3. Add Cheddar cheese and roast for an additional 3 minutes. Serve immediately. Enjoy!

PER SERVING

Calories: 202 | Fat: 16.3g | Carbs: 5.8g | Fiber: 2.3g | Protein: 8.8g

Double-Pork Frittata

Prep time: 5 minutes | Cook time: 25 minutes | Serves 4

- 1 tablespoon butter or pork lard
- 8 large eggs
- 240 ml heavy (whipping) cream
- Pink Himalayan salt
- Freshly ground black pepper
- 113 g pancetta, chopped
- 57 g prosciutto, thinly sliced
- 1 tablespoon chopped fresh dill

1. Preheat the oven to 190°C (375°F). Coat a 9-by-13-inch baking pan with the butter.
2. In a large bowl, whisk the eggs and cream together. Season with pink Himalayan salt and pepper, and whisk to blend.
3. Transfer to a rack to cool for 5 minutes.
4. Cut into 4 portions and serve hot.

PER SERVING

Calories: 437 | Total Fat: 39g | Carbs: 3g | Net Carbs: 3g | Fiber: 0g | Protein: 21g

Indian Masala Frittata

Prep time: 10 minutes | Cook time: 40 minutes |Serves 5

- 2 tablespoons butter
- 8 eggs
- 227 grams cream cheese
- 2 tablespoons milk
- 1 yellow onion, sliced
- 1 bell pepper, chopped
- 1 red chili pepper, chopped
- 1 teaspoon Garam masala
- 1 teaspoon turmeric powder

1. Brush the sides and bottom of a baking pan with 1 tablespoon of melted butter. In a mixing dish, thoroughly combine the eggs, cream cheese, and milk.
2. Then, pour the egg mixture into the baking pan; shake the pan to spread the ingredients evenly.
3. Cut into wedges and serve garnished with coriander leaves. Enjoy!

PER SERVING

Calories: 306 | Fat: 27g | Carbs: 4g | Protein: 12g | Fiber: 0.2g

Bacon Deviled Eggs

Prep time: 5 minutes | Cook time: 15 minutes |Serves 6

- 113 grams bacon, diced
- 10 eggs
- 80 ml Cottage cheese
- 15 ml Dijon mustard
- 1 roasted bell pepper, chopped
- 15 ml coriander, minced

1. Preheat a skillet over medium-high heat. Then, fry the bacon until crisp; reserve.
2. Arrange the eggs in a small saucepan. Pour in water (2.5 cm above the eggs) and bring to a boil.
3. Turn off the heat and let it sit, covered, for 9 to 10 minutes.
4. Mix the egg yolks with the reserved bacon, cheese, mustard, bell pepper, salt, and black pepper. Stuff the eggs, arrange on a nice serving platter, and garnish with fresh coriander. Enjoy!

PER SERVING

Calories: 293| Fat: 22.3g | Carbs: 4.8g | Protein: 18.6g | Fiber: 0.8g

Bacon-Wrapped Avocado Fries

Prep time: 10 minutes | Cook time:18 minutes |Serves 4

- 2 medium Hass avocados, peeled and pitted (about 220 g of flesh)
- 16 strips bacon (about 455 g), cut in half lengthwise

1. Cut each avocado into 8 fry-shaped pieces, making a total of 16 fries.
2. Wrap each avocado fry in 2 half-strips of bacon. Once complete, place in a large frying pan.
3. Set the pan over medium heat and cover with a splash guard. Fry for 6 minutes on each side and on the bottom, or until crispy, for a total of 18 minutes.
4. Remove from the heat and enjoy immediately!

PER SERVING

Calories: 723 | Fat: 58.3 g | Carbs: 6.4 g | Dietary Fiber: 3.7 g | Net Carbs: 2.7 g | Sugars: 0.3 g | Protein: 43.2 g

Paprika Egg Salad

Prep time: 5 minutes | Cook time: 20 minutes | Serves 5

- 7 eggs
- 2 spring onions, chopped
- 250 ml radishes, thinly sliced
- 1 bell pepper, chopped
- 80 ml mayonnaise
- 5 ml wholegrain mustard
- 5 ml paprika

1. Place the eggs in a saucepan. Pour in water (2.5 cm above the eggs) and bring to the boil. Turn off the heat and let it sit, covered, for 13 minutes.
2. Add the spring onions, radishes, bell peppers, mayo, and mustard. Season with sea salt and black pepper to taste. Gently stir until everything is well incorporated.
3. Sprinkle paprika on top and serve well chilled. Enjoy!

PER SERVING

Calories: 172 | Fat: 14.1g | Carbs: 2.5g | Protein: 8.1g | Fiber: 0.7g

The Super British Keto Diet Cookbook

Tart with Broccoli and Greek Yogurt

Prep time: 5 minutes | Cook time: 30 minutes |Serves 4

- 2 teaspoons olive oil
- 1 red onion, sliced
- 400 grams broccoli florets
- 1/2 teaspoon paprika
- 1/4 teaspoon ground cumin
- 6 eggs
- 6 tablespoons Greek yogurt
- 120 grams cheddar cheese, shredded

1. Heat the olive oil in an oven-safe pan over a moderate flame. Then, sauté the onion and broccoli until tender, about 3 minutes.
2. Bake at 180 degrees Celsius (about 360 degrees Fahrenheit) for about 18 minutes or until cooked through. Top with the cheese, switch to broil, and let it cook for 5 minutes more. Enjoy!

PER SERVING

Calories: 308 | Fat: 23.2g | Carbs: 5.3g | Protein: 19.2g | Fiber: 0.9g

Mini Frittatas with Sausage and Goat Cheese

Prep time: 10 minutes | Cook time: 35 minutes |Serves 6

- 170 grams pork sausage, sliced
- 1 teaspoon fresh garlic
- 4 tablespoons spring onions, chopped
- 1 bell pepper, chopped
- 1/2 teaspoon basil
- 1/2 teaspoon oregano
- 150 grams goat cheese, crumbled

1. Heat up a lightly oiled nonstick skillet over a moderate flame. Then, sear the sausage, crumbling it with a fork.
2. Top with the goat cheese and bake for 5 to 7 minutes longer or until they start to get slightly browned on top.
3. You can store these mini frittatas in the refrigerator for up to 4 days and reheat when ready to eat. Enjoy!

PER SERVING

Calories: 287 | Fat: 23.7g | Carbs: 1.9g | Protein: 16.1g | Fiber: 0.2g

Chapter 4

Snacks and Appetizers

Provolone Cheese Chips with Herbs

Prep time: 5 minutes | Cook time: 30 minutes |Serves 5

- 170 grams provolone cheese, grated
- 1/2 teaspoon garlic powder
- 1/2 teaspoon shallot powder
- 1/4 teaspoon ground black pepper
- 1 teaspoon dried dill
- 1/2 teaspoon dried oregano
- 1 teaspoon paprika

1. Place the grated provolone cheese in small heaps on a roasting pan lined with a Silpat mat. Make sure to leave enough room in between them.
2. Sprinkle the herbs and spices over them.
3. Bake in the preheated oven at 200 degrees Celsius (about 395 degrees Fahrenheit) for about 9 minutes. Serve with a homemade salsa sauce if desired.

PER SERVING

Calories: 119 | Fat: 9g | Carbs: 0.7g | Protein: 8.7g | Fiber: 0.2g

Cheesy Chicken and Ham Bites

Prep time: 5 minutes | Cook time: 30 minutes |Serves 5

- 5 slices ham
- 5 chicken fillets, about 0.6 cm thin
- 85 grams Ricotta cheese
- 80 ml Colby cheese, grated
- 120 ml spicy tomato sauce

1. Place a slice of ham on each chicken fillet.
2. Thoroughly combine the Ricotta cheese and Colby cheese until everything is well incorporated.
3. Then, divide the cheese mixture between the chicken fillets. Roll them up and secure with toothpicks.
4. Pour the spicy tomato sauce over the chicken roll-ups and bake for another 4 to 6 minutes or until everything is thoroughly cooked. Enjoy!

PER SERVING

Calories: 289 | Fat: 11.1g | Carbs: 7.2g | Protein: 36.8g | Fiber: 2g

Greek-Style Ricotta Dip with Olives

Prep time: 5 minutes | Cook time: 15 minutes |Serves 10

- 283 grams ricotta cheese
- 4 tablespoons Greek yogurt
- 1/2 teaspoon cayenne pepper
- 4 tablespoons olives, sliced
- 1/2 teaspoon garlic salt
- 1/2 teaspoon black pepper
- 4 tablespoons coriander, minced

1. Thoroughly combine the ricotta cheese, Greek yogurt, cayenne pepper, olives, shallot powder, garlic salt, and black pepper in a mixing bowl.
2. Transfer to a nice serving bowl.
3. Garnish with coriander, serve, and enjoy your party!

PER SERVING

Calories: 72 | Fat: 5.5g | Carbs: 1.9g | Protein: 4.3g | Fiber: 0.2g

Favorite Onions Rings

Prep time: 5 minutes | Cook time: 20 minutes |Serves 4

- 120 grams coconut flour
- 3 eggs
- 2 tablespoons water
- 2 tablespoons double cream
- 113 grams pork rinds
- 85 grams parmesan cheese, grated
- 2 onions, cut into 1.3 cm thick rings

1. Place the coconut flour in a shallow dish. In another dish, mix the eggs, water, and cream; place the pork rinds and parmesan in the third dish.
2. Place the coated rings on a lightly greased baking rack; bake at 220 degrees Celsius (about 420 degrees Fahrenheit) for 13 to 16 minutes. Enjoy!

PER SERVING

Calories: 322 | Fat: 27.8g | Carbs: 5.7g | Protein: 10.1g | Fiber: 1g

Italian Cheese Crisps

Prep time: 5 minutes | Cook time: 10 minutes |Serves 4

- 225 grams sharp Cheddar cheese, grated
- 1/4 teaspoon ground black pepper
- 1/2 teaspoon cayenne pepper
- 1 teaspoon Italian seasoning

1. Start by preheating an oven to 200 degrees Celsius (about 400 degrees Fahrenheit). Line a baking sheet with parchment paper.
2. Mix all of the above ingredients until well combined.
3. Bake in the preheated oven for 8 minutes, until the edges start to brown. Allow the cheese crisps to cool slightly; then, place them on paper towels to drain the excess fat. Enjoy!

PER SERVING

Calories: 134 | Fat: 11.1g | Carbs: 0.4g | Fiber: 0g | Protein: 4.9g

Double Cheese Bites

Prep time: 5 minutes | Cook time: 15 minutes |Serves 10

- 283 grams Swiss cheese, shredded
- 283 grams cottage cheese
- 60 ml sour cream
- 1 tablespoon pickle, minced
- Sea salt and ground black pepper, to season
- 1 teaspoon granulated garlic
- 75 grams pecans, finely chopped

1. Beat the Swiss cheese, cottage cheese, sour cream, minced pickles, and seasonings until everything is well incorporated.
2. Place the mixture for 2 hours in your refrigerator. Form the mixture into bite-sized balls using your hands and a spoon.
3. Roll the cheese balls over the chopped pecans to coat them evenly. Enjoy!

PER SERVING

Calories: 199 | Fat: 15.5g | Carbs: 4.7g | Protein: 11.3g | Fiber: 0.9g

Mouth-Watering Stuffed Mushrooms

Prep time: 5 minutes | Cook time: 45 minutes |Serves 10

- 20 button mushrooms, stalks removed
- 170 grams cream cheese
- 60 ml mayonnaise
- 1/4 teaspoon mustard seeds
- Sea salt and black pepper, to taste

1. Adjust an oven rack to the center position. Brush your mushrooms with nonstick cooking spray and arrange them on a baking sheet.
2. In the meantime, mix the remaining ingredients until well combined. Enjoy!

PER SERVING

Calories: 103 | Fat: 10g | Carbs: 1.9g | Protein: 2.5g | Fiber: 0.4g

Fudge Bars with Almonds

Prep time: 5 minutes | Cook time: 5 minutes |Serves 7

- 150 grams almonds
- 4 tablespoons coconut flakes
- 4 tablespoons cacao powder, no sugar added
- 3 tablespoons coconut oil

1. Process all ingredients in your blender until everything is well combined, scraping down the sides as needed.
2. Press firmly into a parchment-lined rectangular pan.
3. Cut into squares and serve your bars well chilled. Enjoy!

PER SERVING

Calories: 78 | Fat: 6.8g | Carbs: 4.7g | Protein: 0.5g | Fiber: 1g

The Super British Keto Diet Cookbook | 23

Mediterranean-Style Keto Sticks

Prep time: 5 minutes | Cook time: 20 minutes | Serves 4

- 2 eggs, beaten
- 160 grams Romano cheese, grated
- 200 grams mozzarella, shredded
- 2 garlic cloves, crushed
- 1 teaspoon dried rosemary
- 1 teaspoon dried parsley flakes

1. Mix all of the ingredients until everything is well incorporated. Roll the dough out on a parchment-lined baking pan.
2. Bake in the preheated oven at 180 degrees Celsius (about 360 degrees Fahrenheit) for about 13 minutes until golden brown.
3. Cut into sticks and serve at room temperature. Enjoy!

PER SERVING
Calories: 258 | Fat: 12.2g | Carbs: 3.9g | Protein: 32.6g | Fiber: 1g

Rum Chocolate Chip Cookies

Prep time: 5 minutes | Cook time: 10 minutes | Serves 12

- 120 grams coconut butter
- 57 grams butter
- 120 ml almond butter
- 60 ml confectioners' Swerve
- 1 teaspoon rum extract
- 200 grams almond meal
- 200 grams pork rinds, crushed
- 120 grams chocolate chips, sugar-free

1. Microwave the coconut butter, butter, and almond butter until melted.
2. Add in the Swerve and rum extract. After that, add in the almond meal, pork rinds, and chocolate chips.
3. Refrigerate for at least 3 hours so they can firm up completely. Enjoy!

PER SERVING
Calories: 400 | Fat: 40g | Carbs: 4.9g | Protein: 5.4g | Fiber: 2.9g

Easy Classic Cheesecake

Prep time: 5 minutes | Cook time:30 minutes |Serves 8

Crust Ingredients:
- 3 tablespoons coconut oil
- A pinch of salt
- 3 tablespoons xylitol

Filling Ingredients:
- 227 grams cream cheese, at room temperature
- 2 eggs
- 1/2 teaspoon cinnamon powder
- 1 teaspoon ground anise

1. Mix all of the crust ingredients until everything is well incorporated. Press the crust mixture into a lightly greased springform pan.
2. Spread the filling over the prepared crust. Cover with strips of aluminum foil. Enjoy!

PER SERVING

Calories: 256 | Fat: 24.3g | Carbs: 5g | Protein: 6.1g | Fiber: 1.6g

Vanilla Custard Pudding

Prep time: 5 minutes | Cook time:25 minutes |Serves 4

- 2 eggs
- A pinch of flaky salt
- 2 egg yolks
- 1 vanilla pod
- 4 tablespoons granulated Swerve
- 360 ml heavy whipping cream
- 1/4 teaspoon ground cloves
- 1/4 teaspoon ground cinnamon

1. Carefully separate the egg whites from the yolks. Whip the egg whites just until a bit foamy. Add in a pinch of salt and beat the eggs until soft peaks have formed. Set aside.
2. Place in your refrigerator until ready to use.

PER SERVING

Calories: 214 | Fat: 21g | Carbs: 1.7g | Protein: 5g | Fiber: 0g

The Super British Keto Diet Cookbook

Mom's Coffee Fudge

Prep time: 5 minutes | Cook time: 10 minutes |Serves 6

- 113 grams butter
- 60 ml confectioners' Swerve
- 60 ml cocoa powder
- 1/4 teaspoon ground cinnamon
- 1/4 teaspoon ground cloves
- 1 tablespoon instant coffee granules
- 1/2 teaspoon vanilla extract

1. Using a hand mixer, whip the butter and confectioners' Swerve at low speed.
2. Gradually add in the remaining ingredients, beating after each addition. Scrape the batter into a parchment-lined pan.
3. Place in your refrigerator for at least 2 hours. Cut into squares and serve well-chilled. Devour!

PER SERVING

Calories: 144 | Fat: 15.5g | Carbs: 2.1g | Protein: 0.8g | Fiber: 1.1g

Chapter 5

Poultry

Old-Fashioned Chicken Soup

Prep time: 5 minutes | **Cook time:** 55 minutes | **Serves 6**

- 1 rotisserie chicken, shredded
- 1.4 liters water
- 2 tablespoons butter
- 1/2 onion, chopped
- 1 bay leaf
- 1 tablespoon fresh basil, chopped

1. Cook the bones and carcass from a leftover chicken with water over medium-high heat for 15 minutes. Then, reduce to a simmer and cook an additional 15 minutes. Reserve the chicken along with the broth.
2. Let it cool enough to handle, shred the meat into bite-size pieces.
3. Add the reserved chicken, basil, and cabbage. Simmer for an additional 10 to 11 minutes, until the cabbage is tender. Bon appétit!

PER SERVING

Calories: 265 | Fat: 23.8g | Carbs: 4.3g | Fiber: 1.7g | Protein: 9.3g

Lemon Garlic Grilled Chicken Wings

Prep time: 5 minutes | **Cook time:** 25 minutes | **Serves 4**

- 8 chicken wings
- 2 tablespoons ghee, melted

The Marinade:
- 2 garlic cloves, minced
- 2 tablespoons lemon juice
- Salt and ground black pepper, to taste
- 1/2 teaspoon paprika
- 1 teaspoon dried rosemary

1. Thoroughly combine all ingredients for the marinade in a ceramic bowl. Add the chicken wings to the bowl.
2. Cover and allow it to marinate for 1 hour.
3. Then, preheat your grill to medium-high heat. Drizzle melted ghee over the chicken wings. Grill the chicken wings for 20 minutes, turning them periodically.
4. Taste, adjust the seasonings, and serve warm. Enjoy!

PER SERVING

Calories: 131 | Fat: 7.8g | Carbs: 1.8g | Fiber: 0.2g | Protein: 13.4g

Italian-Seasoned Turkey Breasts

Prep time: 5 minutes | **Cook time:** 20 minutes |Serves 5

- 2 eggs
- 240 ml sour cream
- 1 teaspoon Italian seasoning blend
- Kosher salt and ground black pepper, to taste
- 50 grams grated Parmesan cheese
- 900 grams turkey fillets

1. In a mixing bowl, whisk the eggs until frothy and light. Stir in the sour cream and continue whisking until well combined.
2. In another bowl, mix the Italian seasoning blend with the salt, black pepper, and Parmesan cheese; mix to combine well.
3. Cook in the greased frying pan until browned on all sides. Bon appétit!

PER SERVING

Calories: 335 | Fat: 12.8g | Carbs: 5.3g | Protein: 47.7g | Fiber: 0.1g

Pan-Fried Meatballs

Prep time: 5 minutes | **Cook time:** 80 minutes |Serves 4

- 4 spring onions, finely chopped
- 2 spring garlic stalks, chopped
- 2 tablespoons basil, chopped
- 225 grams ground pork
- 225 grams ground turkey
- 1 egg, whisked
- 50 grams Parmesan cheese, grated
- 1 teaspoon dried rosemary
- 1/2 teaspoon mustard powder
- 2 tablespoons olive oil

1. In a mixing bowl, thoroughly combine all ingredients, except for the olive oil. Shape the mixture into small balls.
2. Refrigerate your meatballs for 1 hour.
3. Turn them and cook for 6 minutes on the other side. Bon appétit!

PER SERVING

Calories: 366 | Fat: 27.7g | Carbs: 3g | Protein: 25.9g | Fiber: 0.5g

Buttery Garlic Chicken

Prep time: 5 minutes | Cook time: 40 minutes | Serves 2

- 30 g ghee, melted
- 2 boneless skinless chicken breasts
- Pink Himalayan salt
- Freshly ground black pepper
- 60 g butter
- 2 garlic cloves, minced
- 25 g grated Parmesan cheese

1. Preheat the oven to 190°C (170°C fan). Choose a baking dish that is large enough to hold both chicken breasts and coat it with the melted ghee.
2. Pat dry the chicken breasts and season with pink Himalayan salt, pepper, and Italian seasoning. Place the chicken in the baking dish.
3. Divide the chicken between two plates, spoon the butter sauce over the chicken, and serve.

PER SERVING

Calories: 642 | Total Fat: 45g | Carbs: 2g | Net Carbs: 2g | Fiber: 0g | Protein: 57g

Roast Chicken with Olives

Prep time: 5 minutes | Cook time: 75 minutes | Serves 5

- 900 grams whole chicken
- 1 teaspoon paprika
- 1 teaspoon lemon zest, slivered
- 175 grams oil-cured black olives, pitted
- 4 cloves garlic
- 1 bunch fresh thyme, leaves picked

1. Begin by preheating your oven to 180 degrees Celsius (360 degrees F). Then, spritz the sides and bottom of a baking dish with nonstick cooking oil.
2. Sprinkle the chicken with paprika, lemon zest, salt, and black pepper. Bake for 60 minutes.
3. Scatter black olives, garlic, and thyme around the chicken and bake an additional 10 to 13 minutes; a meat thermometer should read 82 degrees Celsius (180 degrees F). Bon appétit!

PER SERVING

Calories: 235 | Fat: 7.5g | Carbs: 2.7g | Protein: 37.3g | Fiber: 1g

Parmesan Baked Chicken

Prep time: 5 minutes | Cook time: 20 minutes | Serves 2

- 30 g ghee
- 2 boneless skinless chicken breasts
- Pink Himalayan salt
- Freshly ground black pepper
- 120 ml mayonnaise
- 60 g grated Parmesan cheese
- 15 ml dried Italian seasoning
- 30 g crushed pork rinds

1. Preheat the oven to 220°C (200°C fan). Choose a baking dish that is large enough to hold both chicken breasts and coat it with the ghee.
2. In a small bowl, mix to combine the mayonnaise, Parmesan cheese, and Italian seasoning.
3. Bake until the topping is browned, about 20 minutes, and serve.

PER SERVING

Calories: 850 | Total Fat: 67g | Carbs: 2g | Net Carbs: 2g | Fiber: 0g | Protein: 60g

Cheesy Jalapeño Chicken

Prep time: 5 minutes | Cook time: 50 minutes | Serves 4

- 6 boneless, skinless chicken breasts (450 to 675 grams), sliced in half lengthwise
- ½ teaspoon garlic powder
- Pinch of sea salt
- 4 jalapeños
- 170 grams cream cheese, softened
- 200g shredded cheddar cheese

1. Preheat the oven to 190°C (375°F).
2. Dice 3 of the jalapeños. In a small bowl, mix them with the cream cheese. Spread the mixture over the chicken.
3. Remove the foil and bake for 10 minutes, or until the chicken is cooked through and reaches an internal temperature of 74°C (165°F).
4. Thinly slice the last jalapeño and scatter it on top for a fresh kick of heat.

PER SERVING

Calories: 437 | Fat: 28g | Saturated Fat: 15.3g | Protein: 42.3g | Carbs: 2.6g | Fiber: 0.4g | Sodium: 437mg

Green Chicken Curry

Prep time: 5 minutes | Cook time: 12 minutes | Serves 4

- 3 tablespoons green curry paste
- 1 tablespoon coconut oil
- 3 tablespoons granulated erythritol
- 2 tablespoons fish sauce (no sugar added)
- 120 grams sliced yellow bell peppers
- 120 grams sliced bamboo shoots, drained
- 1 tablespoon sliced chili peppers
- Fresh coriander leaves, for garnish

1. Combine the curry paste and coconut oil in a large skillet and cook over medium heat for 2 minutes, or until fragrant.
2. Add the chicken, bell peppers, bamboo shoots, and chili peppers. Simmer, stirring occasionally, for another 5 minutes, and the broccoli is fork-tender. Garnish with coriander and serve hot.

PER SERVING

Calories: 301 | Fat: 20g | Protein: 29g | Carbs: 8g | Fiber: 4g |Net Carbs: 4g

Coconut Chicken Tenders

Prep time: 5 minutes | Cook time: 45 minutes | Serves 3

- 2 tablespoons coconut oil, melted
- 30 grams coconut flour
- 1 teaspoon sea salt
- ¼ teaspoon freshly ground black pepper
- ¼ teaspoon garlic powder
- 2 large eggs, beaten
- 85 grams unsweetened shredded coconut
- 450 grams chicken tenders

1. Preheat the oven to 200°C (400°F). Place a wire rack on a parchment-lined baking sheet and brush with melted coconut oil to prevent sticking.
2. Place the coated tenders on the wire rack. Avoid overcrowding. Bake for 25 minutes, or until the internal temperature reaches 74°C (165°F). Serve warm.

PER SERVING

Calories: 810 | Fat: 57.5g| Protein: 42.3g | Carbs: 29.9g | Fiber: 18.7g | Sodium: 981mg

Chapter 6

Beef, Lamb and Pork

Sunday Pot Roast with Vegetable Mash

Prep time: 5 minutes | Cook time: 1 hour 25 minutes |Serves 5

- 1 teaspoon smoked paprika
- 1/2 teaspoon dried thyme
- 1/2 teaspoon dried rosemary
- 150 grams cauliflower florets
- 227 grams parsnips, chopped
- 2 tablespoons butter

1. Season the chuck roast with the paprika, thyme, rosemary, salt, and black pepper. Place on a foil-lined baking pan.
2. Bake in the preheated oven at 190 degrees Celsius (370 degrees F) for 40 minutes. Let it stand for 15 minutes before slicing and serving.
3. Drain well. Fold in the butter and mash with a potato masher. Serve with the roast beef and enjoy!

PER SERVING

Calories: 324 | Fat: 15.1g | Carbs: 6.5g | Protein: 38.4g | Fiber: 2.8g

Cheesy and Buttery Pork Chops

Prep time: 5 minutes | Cook time: 20 minutes |Serves 2

- 60 grams unsalted butter, room temperature
- 100g white onion, chopped
- 115 grams button mushrooms, sliced
- 150 grams pork loin chops
- 1 teaspoon dried parsley flakes
- Salt and ground black pepper, to taste
- 50 grams Swiss cheese, shredded

1. Melt 1/4 of the butter in a skillet over medium heat. Then, sauté the onions and mushrooms until the onions are translucent and the mushrooms are tender and fragrant, about 5 minutes. Reserve.
2. Then, melt the remaining 1/4 of the butter and cook the pork until slightly browned on all sides, about 10 minutes.
3. Serve immediately and enjoy!

PER SERVING

Calories: 494 | Fat: 39.8g | Carbs: 5.3g | Fiber: 1.1g | Protein: 28.6g

Paprika Crusted Pork Cutlets

Prep time: 5 minutes | Cook time: 15 minutes |Serves 6

- 2 tablespoons vegetable oil
- 2 eggs
- 100 grams Romano cheese, preferably freshly grated
- 1 tablespoon paprika
- 6 pork cutlets
- Sea salt and ground black pepper, to taste

1. Heat the vegetable oil in a large frying pan over a medium-high flame.
2. Working one at a time, dip the pork cutlets into the eggs, then dredge in the Romano cheese mixture, pressing to coat.
3. Fry the pork chops approximately 4 minutes on each side. Transfer to a paper towel-lined plate and serve warm. Bon appétit!

PER SERVING

Calories: 454 | Fat: 21.5g | Carbs: 1.1g | Protein: 60.7g | Fiber: 0.4g

Christmas Chuck Eye Roast

Prep time: 5 minutes | Cook time: 1 hour 35 minutes |Serves 5

- 907 grams chuck eye roast
- 60 ml apple cider vinegar
- 80 ml cream of mushroom soup
- 15 ml Dijon mustard
- Sea salt and freshly cracked black pepper, to taste
- 1 bay laurel
- 1 thyme sprig
- 1 rosemary sprig
- 2 tablespoons fresh chives, chopped

1. Start by preheating your oven to 180 degrees Celsius (350 degrees F).
2. Heat a lightly oiled frying pan over medium-high heat. Sear the roast for 2 to 3 minutes per side; place the roast in a baking pan.
3. Serve garnished with fresh chives. Enjoy!

PER SERVING

Calories: 267 | Fat: 11.4g | Carbs: 2.4g | Protein: 37.8g | Fiber: 0.4g

The Super British Keto Diet Cookbook

Bacon, Pork and Cabbage Skillet

Prep time: 5 minutes | Cook time: 20 minutes | Serves 5

- 140 grams bacon, diced
- 450 grams pork steak, cut into strips
- 4 tablespoons dry white wine
- 1 onion, sliced
- 2 bell peppers, sliced
- 400 grams green cabbage, shredded
- 4 cloves garlic, sliced

1. Preheat a wok or a large pan over medium-high heat. Then, cook the bacon for 4 minutes or until crisp.
2. Add in the wine, onion, and peppers. Stir fry for 4 minutes more. Then stir in the cabbage and garlic; continue stirring for about 3 minutes more.
3. Season with salt and black pepper to taste and serve warm.

PER SERVING

Calories: 314 | Fat: 22.5g | Carbs: 7g | Protein: 20.7g | Fiber: 1.8g

Easy Jerk Ribs

Prep time: 2 minutes | Cook time: 1 hour 45 minutes | Serves 4

- 1 rack baby back ribs
- 60 ml Jerk Seasoning
- 2 teaspoons kosher salt
- 120 ml Easy Keto BBQ Sauce

1. Preheat a grill to medium heat. Generously season the rack of ribs on both sides with the jerk seasoning and salt. The ribs should be browned and crispy looking on the outside.
2. Wrap the ribs loosely in foil and place on the grill over indirect heat. You may need to move coals to the side, or turn off one or two burners to create a flame-free space.
3. with the lid closed, cook the ribs for 1 hour; the grill temperature should be about 180°C. Cut into individual ribs to serve.

PER SERVING

Calories: 390 | Fat: 27g | Protein: 26g | Carbs: 6g | Fiber: 2g |Net Carbs: 4g

Restaurant-Style Burger Patties

Prep time: 5 minutes | Cook time: 30 minutes |Serves 5

- 680 grams ground beef
- 227 grams cheddar cheese, shredded
- Sea salt and freshly cracked black pepper, to season
- 15 ml olive oil

1. Thoroughly combine the ground beef, 113 grams of cheddar cheese, egg, salt, and black pepper. Shape the beef mixture into 5 patties.
2. Heat the olive oil in a nonstick frying pan over medium heat. Cook the burger patties for 7 minutes; turn them over.
3. Divide the remaining cheddar cheese between the patties and bake for a further 7 minutes.
4. Serve on lettuce leaves with mayonnaise if desired. Enjoy!

PER SERVING

Calories: 297 | Fat: 23.6g | Carbs: 0.7g | Protein: 20.2g | Fiber: 0.1g

Classic Oven Pot Roast

Prep time: 5 minutes | Cook time: 2 hours 10 minutes |Serves 6

- 907 grams boneless chuck roast, trimmed
- 8 garlic cloves, halved
- 240 ml beef bone broth
- 120 ml Marsala wine
- 30 ml olive oil
- 120 ml low-carb marinara sauce
- 2.5 ml liquid smoke
- 2.5 ml chipotle powder
- Flaky salt, to taste

1. Lower the boneless chuck roast into a lightly greased baking pan. Now, scatter the garlic cloves around the chuck roast.
2. Roast in the preheated oven at 180 degrees C (360 degrees F) approximately 2 hours.
3. Shred the roast with two forks and serve it with the cooking liquid. Garnish with basil leaves if desired. Bon appétit!

PER SERVING

Calories: 265 | Fat: 13.9g | Carbs: 3.2g | Protein: 31.8g | Fiber: 0.5g

The Super British Keto Diet Cookbook | 37

Sweet Beef Curry

Prep time: 10 minutes | Cook time: 30 minutes |Serves 4

- 455 grams large shrimp, peeled and deveined
- 2 tablespoons avocado oil
- 2 cloves garlic, minced
- 2 teaspoons dried basil
- 1¾ teaspoons paprika

Salad:
- 1 large head butter lettuce, chopped
- 1 medium Hass avocado, peeled, pitted, and sliced (about 110 grams of flesh)

1. Place the shrimp, oil, garlic, basil, thyme, paprika, black pepper, salt, and cayenne in a large frying pan. Toss to coat the shrimp, then turn the heat to pink, about 5 minutes.
2. Add the asparagus, cover, and cook for 10 minutes, or until the asparagus is fork-tender.

PER SERVING

Calories: 698 | Fat: 56 g | Carbs: 16.9 g | Dietary Fiber: 3.5 g | Net Carbs: 13.4 g | Sugars: 5.8 g | Protein: 31.8 g

Pork Fillets with Mustard Sauce

Prep time: 5 minutes | Cook time: 20 minutes |Serves 4

- 60 grams butter, melted
- 450 grams pork fillets
- 2 spring onions, chopped
- 1 teaspoon cayenne pepper
- 1 teaspoon dried basil
- 2 tablespoons whole-grain Dijon mustard
- 2 tablespoons chicken stock

1. Melt the butter in a frying pan over a moderate flame. Now, brown the pork fillets for about 3 minutes per side; reserve.
2. Then, in the pan drippings, continue to cook the spring onions and garlic for a minute or so. Add in a splash of wine to scrape up the browned bits that stick to the bottom of the pan.
3. Spoon the sauce over the pork fillets and serve warm. Bon appétit!

PER SERVING

Calories: 343 | Fat: 17.5g | Carbs: 5.4g | Protein: 40g | Fiber: 1g

BBQ Beef & Slaw

Prep time: 10 minutes | Cook time: 45 minutes or 4 to 6 hours | Serves 4

For the Beef:
- 455 grams beef strips (choose a cut suitable for slow cooking)
- 2 tablespoons vegetable oil
- 2 cloves garlic, minced
- 2 teaspoons dried basil
- 1 teaspoon dried thyme leaves
- 1¾ teaspoons paprika
- ¾ teaspoon ground black pepper
- ½ teaspoon finely ground sea salt
- ⅛ teaspoon cayenne pepper

For the Slaw:
- 1 large head of cabbage, shredded
- 1 medium carrot, grated
- 1 small red onion, thinly sliced
- 1 medium apple, thinly sliced

For the Dressing:
- 120 ml mayonnaise
- 2 tablespoons white wine vinegar
- 1 tablespoon Dijon mustard
- 1 tablespoon honey or a low-carb sweetener alternative
- Salt and pepper to taste

1. In a large frying pan, heat the vegetable oil over medium heat. Add the minced garlic and beef strips. Cook until the beef is browned on all sides.
2. In a small bowl, mix together the dried basil, dried thyme, paprika, black pepper, sea salt, and cayenne pepper. Sprinkle this seasoning mix over the beef and stir to coat evenly. Cook for an additional 5 minutes.
3. If you have time, you can transfer the beef to a slow cooker and cook on low for 4 to 6 hours for a more tender result. If not, continue cooking on the stovetop.
4. Add the asparagus to the pan and cook until the asparagus is fork-tender.
5. For the slaw, combine the shredded cabbage, grated carrot, sliced red onion, and sliced apple in a large bowl.
6. Pour the dressing over the slaw and toss until everything is well coated.
7. Serve the BBQ beef over a bed of slaw and enjoy!

PER SERVING

Calories: 450 | Fat: 30g | Carbs: 10g | Fiber: 6g | Protein: 25g

Chapter 7

Fish and Seafood

Baked Lemon-Butter Fish

Prep time: 10 minutes | Cook time: 20 minutes | Serves 2

- 60 g butter, plus more for coating
- 2 (142 g) tilapia fillets
- Pink Himalayan salt
- Freshly ground black pepper
- 2 garlic cloves, minced
- 1 lemon, zested and juiced
- 30 g capers, rinsed and chopped

1. Preheat the oven to 200°C (180°C fan). Coat an 8-inch baking dish with butter.
2. Pat dry the tilapia with paper towels, and season on both sides with pink Himalayan salt and pepper. Place in the prepared baking dish.
3. Pour the lemon-butter sauce over the fish, and sprinkle the capers around the baking pan.
4. Bake for 12 to 15 minutes, until the fish is just cooked through, and serve.

PER SERVING

Calories: 299 | Total Fat: 26g | Carbs: 5g | Net Carbs: 3g | Fiber: 1g | Protein: 16g

Creamy Dill Salmon

Prep time: 10 minutes | Cook time: 10 minutes | Serves 2

- 30 g ghee, melted
- 2 (170 g) salmon fillets, skin on
- Pink Himalayan salt
- Freshly ground black pepper
- 60 ml mayonnaise
- 1 tablespoon Dijon mustard
- 2 tablespoons minced fresh dill
- Pinch garlic powder

1. Preheat the oven to 230°C (210°C fan). Coat a 22x33 cm baking dish with the melted ghee.
2. Slather the mayonnaise sauce on top of both salmon fillets so that it fully covers the tops.
3. Bake for 7 to 9 minutes, depending on how you like your salmon—7 minutes for medium-rare and 9 minutes for well-done—and serve.

PER SERVING

Calories: 510 | Total Fat: 41g | Carbs: 2g | Net Carbs: 2g | Fiber: 1g | Protein: 33g

The Super British Keto Diet Cookbook

Sautéed Pesto Mahi Mahi

Prep time: 5 minutes | Cook time: 15 minutes | Serves 4

- 120 ml fresh basil, lightly packed
- 120 ml fresh sage, lightly packed
- 120 ml fresh basil, lightly packed
- 120 ml fresh parsley, lightly packed
- 2 garlic cloves
- 60 g pine nuts
- 1 lemon, halved

1. Combine the basil, sage, basil, parsley, garlic, oil, and pine nuts in a food processor, and process until the mixture is creamy. Pulse in the Parmesan.
2. When the fish is done, brush both sides with pesto again. Squeeze the lemon over the fish and serve immediately.

PER SERVING

Calories: 511 | Fat: 40.7g | Saturated Fat: 10g | Protein: 36.8g | Carbs: 3.5g | Fiber: 0.9g | Sodium: 239mg

Grilled Garlic-Lemon Prawns

Prep time: 15 minutes | Cook time: 10 minutes | Serves 3

- 300g king prawns, peeled and deveined
- 3 cloves garlic, minced
- Zest of 1 lemon
- 3 tablespoons olive oil
- Pink Himalayan salt, to taste
- Freshly ground black pepper, to taste
- Fresh parsley, chopped (for garnish)

1. In a bowl, combine prawns, minced garlic, lemon zest, and olive oil. Season with salt and pepper.
2. Preheat the grill to medium-high heat.
3. Thread prawns onto skewers and grill for about 2-3 minutes per side, until opaque.
4. Garnish with chopped parsley and serve.

PER SERVING

Calories: 220 | Total Fat: 15g | Carbs: 2g | Net Carbs: 1g | Fiber: 1g | Protein: 18g

Grilled Salmon with Dijon Glaze

Prep time: 10 minutes | **Cook time:** 15 minutes | Serves 3

- 480g salmon fillets
- 2 tablespoons Dijon mustard
- 1 tablespoon honey
- 1 tablespoon olive oil
- 1 clove garlic, minced
- Pink Himalayan salt
- Freshly ground black pepper
- Fresh dill, for garnish

1. Preheat the grill to medium heat.
2. In a bowl, whisk together Dijon mustard, honey, olive oil, and minced garlic.
3. Grill for about 6-8 minutes per side or until the salmon is cooked to your liking.
4. Garnish with fresh dill before serving.

PER SERVING

Calories: 320 | Total Fat: 18g | Carbs: 7g | Net Carbs: 6g | Fiber: 1g | Protein: 30g

Shrimp Scampi with Courgette Noodles

Prep time: 15 minutes | **Cook time:** 10 minutes | Serves 4

- 500g shrimp, peeled and deveined
- 3 tablespoons olive oil
- 3 cloves garlic, minced
- Zest of 1 lemon
- 2 tablespoons fresh parsley, chopped
- 2 large courgettes, spiralized
- Pink Himalayan salt
- Freshly ground black pepper
- Grated Parmesan cheese, for serving

1. Heat olive oil in a pan over medium heat. Add minced garlic and cook until fragrant.
2. Add shrimp and cook for 2-3 minutes on each side until opaque.
3. Stir in lemon zest and fresh parsley.

PER SERVING

Calories: 280 | Total Fat: 16g | Carbs: 4g | Net Carbs: 6g | Fiber: 4g | Protein: 24g

Garlic Butter Prawns

Prep time: 10 minutes | Cook time: 10 minutes | Serves 2

- 300g large prawns, peeled and deveined
- 3 tablespoons unsalted butter
- 4 cloves garlic, minced
- 1 tablespoon fresh parsley, chopped
- 1 teaspoon lemon juice
- Pink Himalayan salt
- Freshly ground black pepper

1. Heat butter in a pan over medium heat. Add minced garlic and sauté until fragrant.
2. Add prawns to the pan and cook for 2-3 minutes on each side until they turn pink.
3. Stir in fresh parsley and lemon juice.
4. Season with salt and pepper.
5. Serve the garlic butter prawns hot.

PER SERVING

Calories: 220 | Total Fat: 15g | Carbs: 1g | Net Carbs: 1g | Fiber: 0g | Protein: 22g

Baked Cod with Herbed Butter

Prep time: 10 minutes | Cook time: 15 minutes | Serves 2

- 2 (150g) cod fillets
- 2 tablespoons unsalted butter, melted
- 1 tablespoon fresh parsley, chopped
- 1 teaspoon fresh dill, chopped
- Pink Himalayan salt
- Lemon wedges, for serving

1. Preheat the oven to 200°C (180°C fan).
2. Place cod fillets in a baking dish.
3. Brush the herbed butter over the cod fillets, ensuring they are well-coated.
4. Season with salt and pepper.
5. Bake for 12-15 minutes or until the cod flakes easily with a fork.
6. Serve with lemon wedges.

PER SERVING

Calories: 260 | Total Fat: 15g | Carbs: 1g | Net Carbs: 1g | Fiber: 0g | Protein: 30g

Grilled Salmon with Dijon-Honey Glaze

Prep time: 15 minutes | Cook time: 10 minutes | Serves 4

- 380g salmon fillets
- 2 tablespoons Dijon mustard
- 1 tablespoon honey
- 1 tablespoon olive oil
- 1 teaspoon lemon juice
- 1 teaspoon fresh thyme, chopped
- Pink Himalayan salt
- Freshly ground black pepper

1. Preheat the grill to medium-high heat.
2. Season salmon fillets with salt and pepper.
3. Brush the Dijon-honey glaze over the salmon.
4. Grill the salmon for 4-5 minutes per side or until it flakes easily.
5. Serve immediately.

PER SERVING

Calories: 320 | Total Fat: 18g | Carbs: 4g | Net Carbs: 8g | Fiber: 0g | Protein: 30g

Lemon Herb Butter Shrimp

Prep time: 10 minutes | Cook time: 5 minutes | Serves 4

- 500g large shrimp, peeled and deveined
- 3 tablespoons unsalted butter
- 2 cloves garlic, minced
- 1 tablespoon fresh parsley, chopped
- 1 tablespoon fresh chives, chopped
- 1 teaspoon lemon zest
- Pink Himalayan salt
- Freshly ground black pepper

1. In a pan, melt butter over medium heat. Add minced garlic and sauté until fragrant.
2. Add shrimp to the pan and cook for 2-3 minutes on each side until they turn pink.
3. Stir in chopped parsley, chives, and lemon zest.
4. Season with salt and pepper.
5. Serve the lemon herb butter shrimp hot.

PER SERVING

Calories: 240 | Total Fat: 16g | Carbs: 2g | Net Carbs: 2g | Fiber: 0g | Protein: 23g

Chapter 8

Vegan and Vegetarian

Radical Radish Chips

Prep time: 10 minutes | Cook time: 20 minutes |Serves 2

- 1 (450-gram) bag radishes
- 350 ml coconut oil, for deep-frying
- ¾ teaspoon pink Himalayan salt
- ½ teaspoon ground black pepper

1. Using a sharp knife, cut the root ends off the radishes, then slice the radishes into thin chips. Place in a bowl and set aside.
2. Heat the coconut oil in a medium-sized saucepan over medium-high heat until the temperature reaches between 165°C and 175°C on a deep-fry thermometer.
3. Once all the chips are fried, season with the salt and pepper. Toss to coat and enjoy immediately!

PER SERVING

Calories: 37 | Fat: 0 g | Protein: 1.5 g | Carbs: 7.5g | Fiber: 3.5 g

Cauliflower and Broccoli Bake

Prep time: 15 minutes | Cook time: 25 minutes | Serves 4

- 1 small cauliflower, cut into florets
- 1 broccoli crown, cut into florets
- 200ml heavy cream
- 100g cream cheese
- 200g cheddar cheese, shredded
- 2 cloves garlic, minced
- Salt and pepper to taste
- Fresh parsley for garnish

1. Preheat the oven to 200°C (180°C fan).
2. Steam cauliflower and broccoli until slightly tender.
3. In a saucepan, heat heavy cream and cream cheese until smooth.
4. Bake for 20 minutes with fresh parsley.

PER SERVING

Calories: 320 | Total Fat: 26g | Carbs: 10g | Net Carbs: 6g | Fiber: 4g | Protein: 10g

The Super British Keto Diet Cookbook

Mixed-Vegetable Lasagna

Prep time: 20 minutes | Cook time: 7 to 8 Hours | Serves 6

- 3 tablespoons extra-virgin olive oil, divided
- 150 grams sliced mushrooms
- 500 ml simple marinara sauce
- 100 grams shredded kale
- 1 tablespoon chopped basil
- 225 grams ricotta cheese
- 225 grams goat cheese
- 200 grams shredded mozzarella cheese

1. Lightly grease the insert of the slow cooker with 1 tablespoon olive oil.
2. Stir the marinara sauce into the mushrooms and stir to combine.
3. Cover and cook on low for 7 to 8 hours.
4. Serve warm.

PER SERVING:

Calories: 345|Total Fat: 25g|Protein: 21g|Total Carbs: 10g|Fiber: 3g|Net Carbs: 7g|Cholesterol: 56mg

Vegan Avocado and Courgette Noodles

Prep time: 15 minutes | Cook time: 10 minutes | Serves 2

- 2 large avocados
- 2 medium courgettes, spiralized
- 200g cherry tomatoes, halved
- 50g fresh basil, chopped
- 2 tablespoons olive oil
- Juice of 1 lemon
- Salt and pepper to taste
- 30g pine nuts, toasted (for garnish)

1. Scoop out the flesh of the avocados and mash in a bowl.
2. Mix in mashed avocado, olive oil, and lemon juice.
3. Season with salt and pepper. Garnish with toasted pine nuts.

PER SERVING

Calories: 380 | Total Fat: 32g | Carbs: 20g | Net Carbs: 8g | Fiber: 12g | Protein: 6g

Baked Courgette Fries

Prep time: 5 minutes | Cook time: 40 minutes | Serves 2

- 1 large or 2 small courgettes
- 60g almond flour
- 1 teaspoon paprika
- ½ teaspoon sea salt
- 1 large egg

1. Preheat the oven to 375°F (190°C). Line a baking sheet with parchment paper.
2. Slice the courgette into "fries." Set them on a paper towel to drain for 5 minutes.
3. In a small bowl, mix together the almond flour, paprika, and salt. In another bowl, whisk the egg.
4. Bake for 15 minutes. Carefully flip them and bake for 10 minutes, or until golden brown.
5. Serve warm.

PER SERVING

Calories: 80 | Fat: 4.4g | Saturated Fat: 0.9g | Protein: 5.6g | Carbs: 6.9g | Fiber: 2.6g | Sodium: 174mg

Carrot-Pumpkin Pudding

Prep time: 15 minutes | Cook time: 6 Hours | Serves 6

- 1 tablespoon extra-virgin olive oil or ghee
- 450 grams finely shredded carrots
- 450 grams puréed pumpkin
- 1/2 sweet onion, finely chopped
- 240 ml double cream
- 115 grams cream cheese, softened
- 2 eggs
- 1 tablespoon granulated erythritol
- 1 teaspoon ground nutmeg
- 25 grams pumpkin seeds, for garnish

1. Lightly grease the insert of the slow cooker with the olive oil or ghee.
2. Cover and cook on low for 6 hours.
3. Serve warm, topped with the pumpkin seeds.

PER SERVING

Calories: 239 | Total Fat: 19g | Protein: 6g | Total Carbs: 11g | Fiber: 4g | Net Carbs: 7g | Cholesterol: 103mg

The Super British Keto Diet Cookbook

Cheesy Broccoli

Prep time: 5 minutes | **Cook time:** 30 minutes | Serves 4

- 1 pound broccoli florets (fresh or frozen)
- 4 tablespoons grass-fed butter, ghee, or coconut oil
- ½ teaspoon sea salt
- 200g shredded cheddar cheese
- 50g freshly grated Parmesan cheese

1. Preheat the oven to 400°F (200°C).
2. Bring 1 inch of water to a boil in a large pot over medium-high heat. Add in the broccoli, cover, and cook for 5 minutes.
3. Add the butter and mix it together well. Top with the salt and cheese.
4. Bake for 20 minutes, or until the cheese begins to brown.

PER SERVING

Calories: 297 | Fat: 25.1g | Saturated Fat: 18.9g | Protein: 12.9g | Carbs: 8.2g | Fiber: 3g | Sodium: 525mg

Vegan Coconut Curry with Tofu

Prep time: 15 minutes | **Cook time:** 25 minutes | Serves 4

- 200g firm tofu, cubed
- 1 tablespoon coconut oil
- 1 onion, diced
- 2 bell peppers, sliced
- 250g broccoli florets
- 1 tablespoon soy sauce
- 1 tablespoon lime juice
- Fresh basil for garnish

1. In a pan, sauté tofu cubes in coconut oil until golden brown. Set aside.
2. In the same pan, add diced onion and sliced bell peppers. Cook until softened.
3. Simmer for 15 minutes. Garnish with fresh basil.

PER SERVING

Calories: 320 | Total Fat: 25g | Carbs: 12g | Net Carbs: 8g | Fiber: 4g | Protein: 10g

Roasted Radishes

Prep time: 5 minutes | Cook time: 45 minutes | Serves 4

- 2 bunches red radishes
- 1 tablespoon avocado oil
- 2 teaspoons dried thyme
- 1 teaspoon sea salt

1. Preheat the oven to 425°F (220°C).
2. Stem and clean the radishes.
3. Slice them in half and toss in the avocado oil, thyme, and salt. Place on a baking sheet.
4. Roast in the oven for 40 minutes, stirring them halfway through.
5. Serve warm.

PER SERVING

Calories: 15 | Fat: 0.5g | Saturated Fat: 0.1g | Protein: 0.5g | Carbs: 2.5g | Fiber: 1.3g | Sodium: 150mg

Keto Aubergine Parmesan

Prep time: 20 minutes | Cook time: 25 minutes | Serves 4

- 1 large aubergine, sliced
- 2 eggs, beaten
- 100g almond flour
- 200g mozzarella cheese, shredded
- 50g Parmesan cheese, grated
- Fresh basil for garnish

1. Preheat the oven to 200°C (180°C fan).
2. Dip aubergine slices in beaten eggs, then coat with a mixture of almond flour and Italian seasoning.
3. Bake for an additional 10 minutes, or until cheese is melted and bubbly.
4. Garnish with fresh basil.

PER SERVING

Calories: 280 | Total Fat: 20g | Carbs: 2g | Net Carbs: 6g | Fiber: 6g | Protein: 14g

The Super British Keto Diet Cookbook

Chapter 9

Soups, Stew and Salads

Pan-Fried Egg Salad

Prep time: 5 minutes | Cook time:15 minutes |Serves 4

- 2 tablespoons canola oil
- 4 eggs
- 600g lettuce, broken into pieces
- 1 bell pepper, sliced
- 1 red onion, sliced
- 1 avocado, pitted, peeled, and sliced
- 227 grams goat cheese, crumbled

1. Heat the canola oil in a frying pan over the highest heat. Once hot, carefully crack the eggs into the oil. Cook for 1 minute and flip the eggs using a wide spatula.
2. Fry the eggs until the yolks are set; reserve.
3. Mix the lettuce, cucumber, bell pepper, onion, and avocado in a serving bowl. Top with the fried eggs. Garnish with goat cheese and serve immediately. Enjoy!

PER SERVING

Calories: 474 | Fat: 38g | Carbs: 6.3g | Protein: 24g | Fiber: 4.2g

Creamy Cucumber Avocado Soup

Prep time: 5 minutes | Cook time: 5 minutes | Serves 4

- ½ cucumber, peeled
- 1 ripe avocado
- 5 celery stalks
- 3 tablespoons lemon juice
- 60 to 120 ml water
- 1 teaspoon sea salt
- ½ teaspoon freshly ground black pepper
- 57 g raw cheddar cheese or goat feta cheese, shredded

1. Blend all the ingredients except the cheese together in a high-speed blender, using as much water as needed to achieve the desired consistency.
2. Serve chilled topped with the cheese.

PER SERVING

Calories: 172 | Fat: 14.7g | Saturated Fat: 5.2g | Protein: 5g | Carbs: 6.9g | Fiber: 4g | Sodium: 580mg

Shrimp Caprese Salad

Prep time: 12 minutes, plus 30 minutes to chill | Serves 4

- 450 grams large shrimp, peeled, deveined, and cooked
- 240 ml halved cherry tomatoes
- 115 grams fresh mozzarella, cut into 2.5 cm cubes
- 2 tablespoons chopped fresh basil, plus more for garnish if desired
- 1 batch Creamy Basil-Parmesan Vinaigrette
- Instructions:

1. Cut the shrimp in half lengthwise and place in a medium-sized salad bowl.
2. Add the tomatoes, mozzarella, and basil to the bowl. Pour the vinaigrette over the salad ingredients and toss to coat.
3. For best flavor, chill for 30 minutes before serving. Garnish the salad with additional chopped basil if desired.

PER SERVING

Calories: 371 | Fat: 27g | Protein: 30g | Carbs: 3g | Fiber: 1g | Net Carbs: 2g

Shrimp and Avocado Salad

Prep time: 5 minutes | Cook time: 2 minutes | Serves 2

- 15 ml olive oil
- 454 g shrimp (I use defrosted Trader Joe's Frozen Medium Cooked Shrimp, which are peeled and deveined, with tail off)
- Pink Himalayan salt
- Freshly ground black pepper
- 1 avocado, cubed
- 1 celery stalk, chopped
- 60 ml mayonnaise

1. In a large skillet over medium heat, heat the olive oil. When the oil is hot, pink, 1 to 2 minutes. Season with pink Himalayan salt and pepper.
2. Transfer the shrimp to a medium bowl, cover, and refrigerate.
3. Cover the salad, and refrigerate to chill for 30 minutes before serving.

PER SERVING

Calories: 571 | Total Fat: 41g | Carbs: 8g | Net Carbs: 3g | Fiber: 5g | Protein: 50g

Creamy Tomato-Basil Soup

Prep time: 5 minutes | **Cook time:** 15 minutes | **Serves 4**

- 1 (14.5-ounce) can diced tomatoes (I use Muir Glen Organic Tomatoes with Italian Seasonings)
- 57 g cream cheese
- 60 ml heavy (whipping) cream
- 4 tablespoons butter
- 60 ml chopped fresh basil leaves
- Pink Himalayan salt
- Freshly ground black pepper

1. Pour the tomatoes with their juices into a food processor (or blender) and purée until smooth.
2. In a medium saucepan over medium heat, cook the tomatoes, cream cheese, heavy cream, and butter for 10 minutes, stirring occasionally, until all is melted and thoroughly combined.
3. Pour the soup into four bowls and serve.

PER SERVING

Calories: 239 | Total Fat: 22g | Carbs: 9g | Net Carbs: 7g | Fiber: 2g | Protein: 3g

Cabbage Detox Soup

Prep time: 5 minutes | **Cook time:** 1 hour, 20 minutes | **Serves 8**

- 15 ml avocado oil
- 1 yellow onion, diced
- 240 ml diced celery
- 240 ml diced green bell pepper
- 15 ml minced fresh turmeric
- 15 ml minced fresh ginger
- 5 ml freshly ground black pepper
- 15 ml sea salt

1. Heat the avocado oil in a large pot over medium heat.
2. Add the onion, celery, bell pepper, garlic, turmeric, and ginger. Sauté for 5 to 7 minutes, or until the vegetables have softened. Stir in the black pepper and a pinch of the salt.
3. Add the cabbage and sauté for 1 to 2 minutes. Stir in another pinch of salt.

PER SERVING

Calories: 63 | Fat: 0.3g | Saturated Fat: 0.1g | Protein: 7.3g | Carbs: 8.3g | Fiber: 2.2g | Sodium: 236mg

Cajun Shrimp Salad

Prep time: 5 minutes | Cook time: 15 minutes |Serves 4

- 455 grams large shrimp, peeled and deveined
- 2 tablespoons avocado oil
- 2 cloves garlic, minced
- 2 teaspoons dried basil
- 1 teaspoon dried thyme leaves
- 120 ml creamy Italian dressing or other creamy salad dressing of choice

1. Place the shrimp, oil, garlic, basil, thyme, paprika, black pepper, salt, and cayenne in a large frying pan. Toss to coat the shrimp, then turn the heat to medium and cook until the shrimp is pink, about 5 minutes.
2. Add the asparagus, cover, and cook for 10 minutes, or until the asparagus is fork-tender.

PER SERVING

Calories: 485 | Fat: 31 g | Carbs: 19.4 g | Dietary Fiber: 7.2 g | Net Carbs: 12.2 g | Protein: 32.2 g

Blue Cheese and Bacon Kale Salad

Prep time: 10 minutes | Cook time: 10 minutes | Serves 2

- 4 bacon slices
- 474 ml stemmed and chopped fresh kale
- 15 ml vinaigrette salad dressing (I use Primal Kitchen Greek Vinaigrette)
- Pinch pink Himalayan salt
- Pinch freshly ground black pepper
- 60 ml blue cheese crumbles

1. In a medium skillet over medium-high heat, cook the bacon on both sides until crispy, about 8 minutes. Transfer the bacon to a paper towel–lined plate.
2. Chop the bacon and pecans, and add them to the bowl. Sprinkle in the blue cheese.
3. Toss well to combine, portion onto two plates, and serve.

PER SERVING

Calories: 353 | Total Fat: 29g | Carbs: 10g | Net Carbs: 7g | Fiber: 3g | Protein: 16g

Cheeseburger Salad

Prep time: 10 minutes | Cook time: 10 minutes | Serves 2

- 15 ml ghee
- 450 g ground beef
- Pink Himalayan salt
- Freshly ground black pepper
- 120 ml finely chopped dill pickles
- 120 g shredded Cheddar cheese
- 30 ml ranch salad dressing

1. In a medium skillet over medium-high heat, heat the ghee.
2. Put the pickles in a large bowl, and add the romaine and cheese.
3. Using a slotted spoon, transfer the browned beef from the skillet to the bowl.
4. Top the salad with the dressing, and toss to thoroughly coat.
5. Divide into two bowls and serve.

PER SERVING

Calories: 662 | Total Fat: 50g | Carbs: 6g | Net Carbs: 4g | Fiber: 2g | Protein: 47g

Taco Soup

Prep time: 5 minutes | Cook time: 4 hours 10 minutes| Serves 4

- 454 g ground beef
- Pink Himalayan salt
- Freshly ground black pepper
- 480 ml beef broth (I use Kettle & Fire Bone Broth)
- 283 g can diced tomatoes (I use Rotel)
- 15 ml taco seasoning
- 227 g cream cheese

1. with the crock insert in place, preheat the slow cooker to low.
2. Add the ground beef, beef broth, tomatoes, taco seasoning, and cream cheese to the slow cooker.
3. Cover and cook on low for 4 hours, stirring occasionally.
4. Ladle into four bowls and serve.

PER SERVING

Calories: 422 | Total Fat: 33g | Carbs: 6g | Net Carbs: 5g | Fiber: 1g | Protein: 25g

Appendix 1 Measurement Conversion Chart

Volume Equivalents (Dry)	
US STANDARD	METRIC (APPROXIMATE)
1/8 teaspoon	0.5 mL
1/4 teaspoon	1 mL
1/2 teaspoon	2 mL
3/4 teaspoon	4 mL
1 teaspoon	5 mL
1 tablespoon	15 mL
1/4 cup	59 mL
1/2 cup	118 mL
3/4 cup	177 mL
1 cup	235 mL
2 cups	475 mL
3 cups	700 mL
4 cups	1 L

Volume Equivalents (Liquid)		
US STANDARD	US STANDARD (OUNCES)	METRIC (APPROXIMATE)
2 tablespoons	1 fl.oz.	30 mL
1/4 cup	2 fl.oz.	60 mL
1/2 cup	4 fl.oz.	120 mL
1 cup	8 fl.oz.	240 mL
1 1/2 cup	12 fl.oz.	355 mL
2 cups or 1 pint	16 fl.oz.	475 mL
4 cups or 1 quart	32 fl.oz.	1 L
1 gallon	128 fl.oz.	4 L

Temperatures Equivalents	
FAHRENHEIT(F)	CELSIUS(C) APPROXIMATE)
225 °F	107 °C
250 °F	120 ° °C
275 °F	135 °C
300 °F	150 °C
325 °F	160 °C
350 °F	180 °C
375 °F	190 °C
400 °F	205 °C
425 °F	220 °C
450 °F	235 °C
475 °F	245 °C
500 °F	260 °C

Weight Equivalents	
US STANDARD	METRIC (APPROXIMATE)
1 ounce	28 g
2 ounces	57 g
5 ounces	142 g
10 ounces	284 g
15 ounces	425 g
16 ounces (1 pound)	455 g
1.5 pounds	680 g
2 pounds	907 g

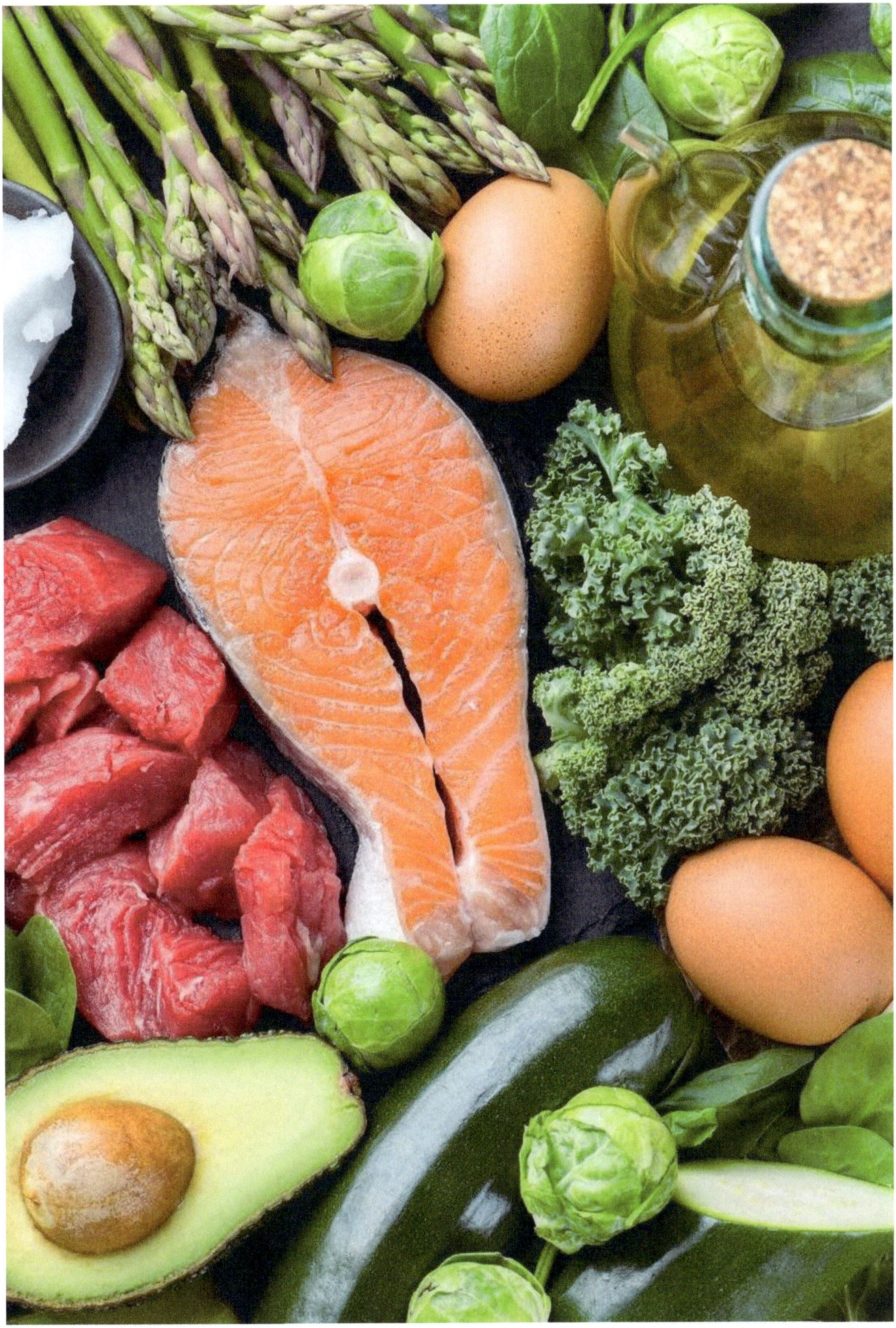

Appendix 2 The Dirty Dozen and Clean Fifteen

The Environmental Working Group (EWG) is a nonprofit, nonpartisan organization dedicated to protecting human health and the environment Its mission is to empower people to live healthier lives in a healthier environment. This organization publishes an annual list of the twelve kinds of produce, in sequence, that have the highest amount of pesticide residue-the Dirty Dozen-as well as a list of the fifteen kinds of produce that have the least amount of pesticide residue-the Clean Fifteen.

THE DIRTY DOZEN

The 2016 Dirty Dozen includes the following produce. These are considered among the year's most important produce to buy organic:

Strawberries	Spinach
Apples	Tomatoes
Nectarines	Bell peppers
Peaches	Cherry tomatoes
Celery	Cucumbers
Grapes	Kale/collard greens
Cherries	Hot peppers

The Dirty Dozen list contains two additional items kale/collard greens and hot peppers-because they tend to contain trace levels of highly hazardous pesticides.

THE CLEAN FIFTEEN

The least critical to buy organically are the Clean Fifteen list. The following are on the 2016 list:

Avocados	Papayas
Corn	Kiw
Pineapples	Eggplant
Cabbage	Honeydew
Sweet peas	Grapefruit
Onions	Cantaloupe
Asparagus	Cauliflower
Mangos	

Some of the sweet corn sold in the United States are made from genetically engineered (GE) seedstock. Buy organic varieties of these crops to avoid GE produce.

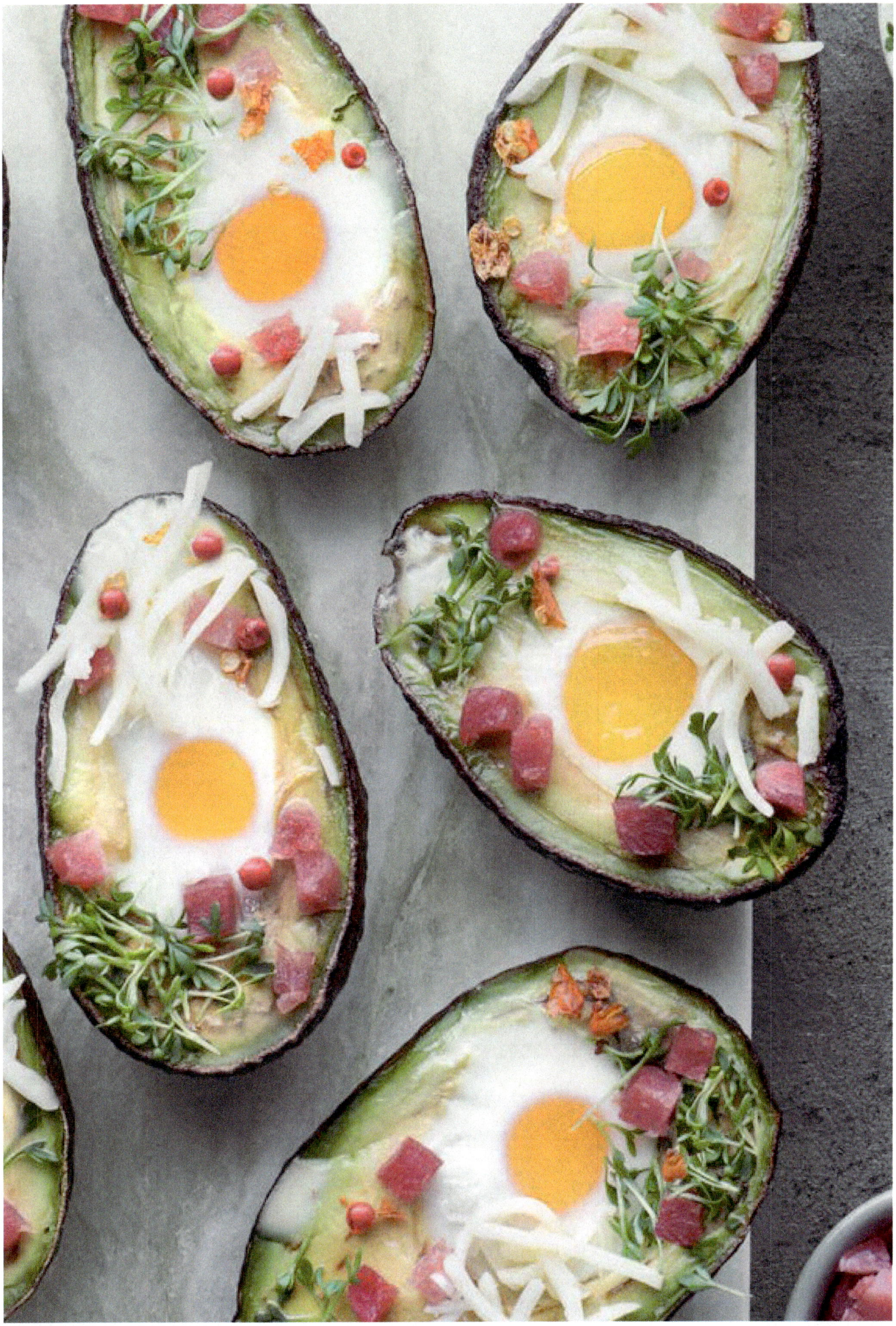

Appendix 3 Index

A

almond 14, 24, 49, 51
apple 35, 39
apple cider vinegar 35
avocado 17, 38, 48, 51, 53, 54, 55, 56
avocado oil 38, 51, 55, 56

B

bacon 16, 17, 36, 56
basil 18, 28, 29, 37, 38, 39, 42, 48, 50, 51, 54
beef 34, 37, 39, 57
bell pepper 16, 17, 18, 53, 55
black pepper 14, 15, 16, 17, 20, 21, 22, 23
broccoli 18, 32, 47, 50
broccoli florets 18, 50
butter 15, 16, 24, 26, 28, 30, 34, 38

C

canola oil 53
cauliflower 34, 47
cayenne 21, 22, 38, 39, 56
cayenne pepper 21, 22, 38, 39
Cheddar cheese 15, 22, 57
cheese 14, 15, 16, 18, 20, 21, 22, 23, 24, 25
cherry tomatoes 48, 54
chives 35, 45

cinnamon 25, 26
coconut 21, 23, 24, 25, 32, 47, 50
coriander 16, 21, 32

D

Dijon mustard 16, 35, 38, 39, 41, 43, 45
dried basil 38, 39, 56
dried rosemary 24, 28, 29, 34
dried thyme 15, 34, 39, 51, 56

E

egg 16, 25, 29, 37, 49
erythritol 32, 49

F

firm tofu 50
florets 18, 34, 47, 50
flour 14, 21, 32, 49, 51
fresh basil 28, 42, 48, 50, 51, 54, 55
fresh ginger 55
fresh parsley 42, 43, 44, 45, 47

G

garlic 14, 18, 20, 21, 22, 24, 28
garlic powder 20, 31, 32, 41
Greek yogurt 18, 21

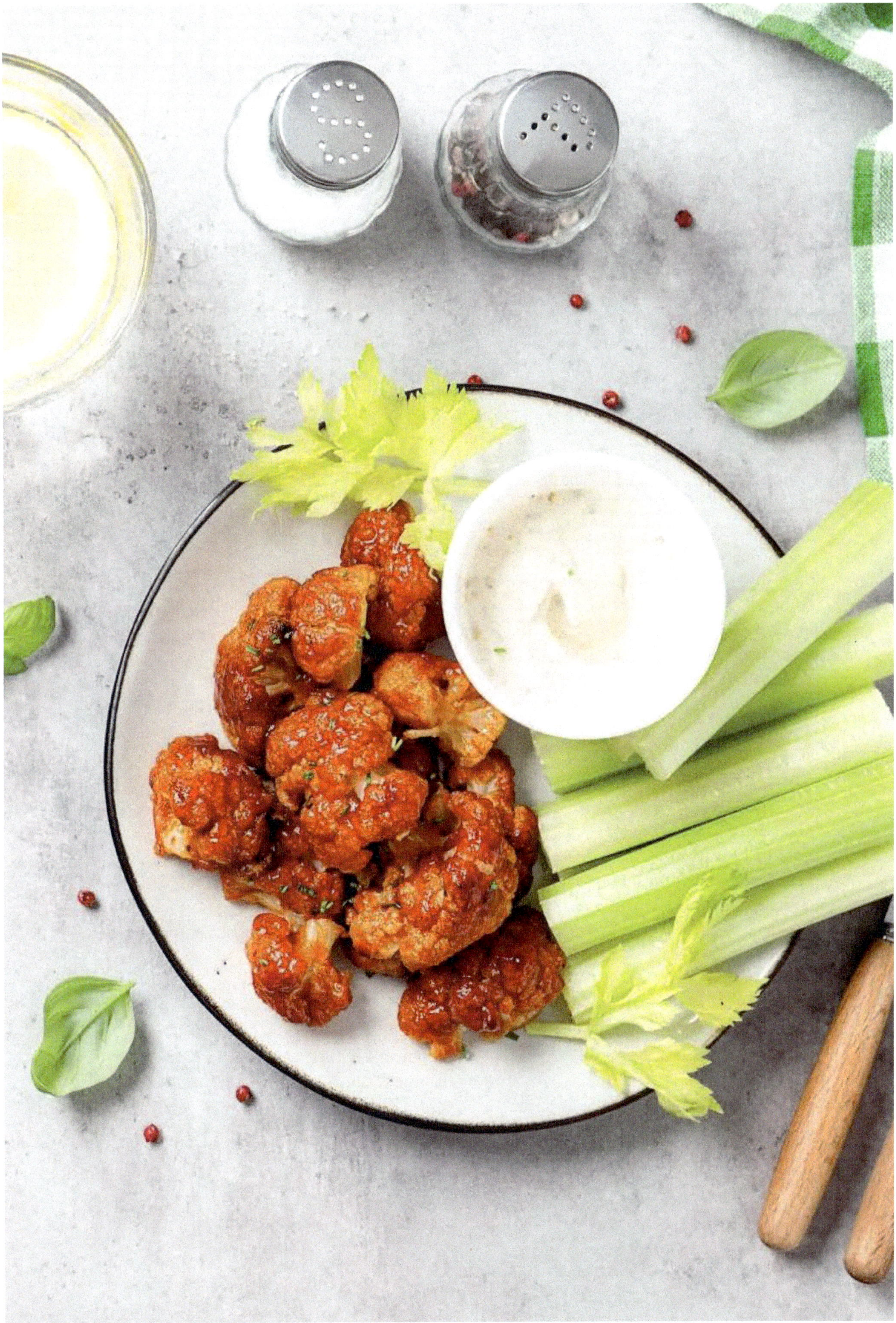

H

Himalayan salt 15, 30, 31, 41, 42, 43, 44, 45, 47, 54, 55, 56, 57
honey 39, 43, 45

J

juice 28, 44, 45, 48, 50, 53

K

kale 48, 56
kosher salt 36

L

large shrimp 38, 45, 54, 56
lemon 28, 30, 41, 42, 43, 44, 45, 48, 53
lemon juice 28, 44, 45, 48, 53
lime 50

M

mayonnaise 17, 23, 31, 37, 39, 41, 54
milk 16
mozzarella 24, 48, 51, 54
mozzarella cheese 48, 51
mustard 14, 16, 17, 23, 29, 35, 38, 39, 41, 43, 45

N

nutmeg 49
nuts 42, 48

O

oil 15, 18, 23, 25, 29, 30, 32, 35, 37, 38
olive oil 18, 29, 37, 42, 43, 45, 48

O (cont.)

onion 16, 18, 28, 34, 36, 39, 49, 50, 53, 55

P

paprika 17, 18, 20, 28, 30, 34, 35, 38, 39, 49, 56
Parmesan cheese 29, 30, 31, 43, 50, 51
parsley 15, 24, 34, 42, 43, 44, 45, 47
pumpkin 49

R

ricotta cheese 21, 48

S

salt 14, 15, 16, 17, 21, 22, 23, 25, 29, 30
sauce 20, 30, 32, 37, 38, 41
soy sauce 50
sugar 23, 24, 32

T

thyme 15, 30, 34, 35, 38, 39, 45, 51
turmeric 16, 55

U

unsalted butter 34, 44, 45

V

vanilla 25, 26
vegetable 35, 39
vinegar 35, 39

Y

yogurt 18, 21

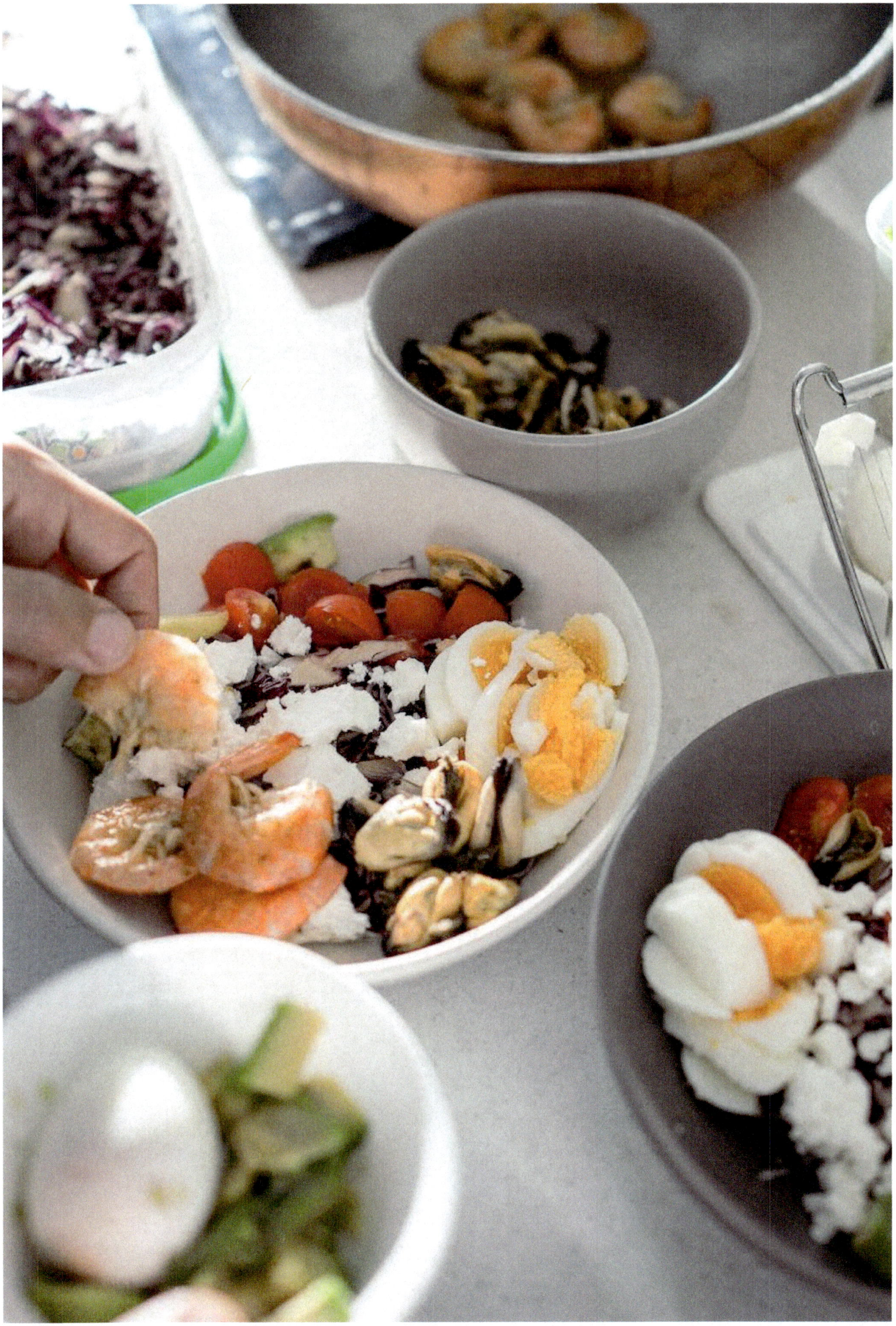

Matilda Nicholson

Printed in Great Britain
by Amazon